# ARCHERY

## Steps to Success

### Second Edition

**Kathleen M. Haywood, PhD**
University of Missouri—St. Louis

**Catherine F. Lewis, MEd**
Andrews Academy
Creve Coeur, Missouri

**Human Kinetics**

Library of Congress Cataloging-in-Publication Data

Haywood, Kathleen.
    Archery : steps to success / Kathleen M. Haywood, Catherine F.
Lewis. -- 2nd ed.
        p.   cm. -- (Steps to success activity series)
    ISBN 0-87322-854-5
    1. Archery.   I. Lewis, Catherine, 1957- .   II. Title.
III. Series.
GV1185.H38   1997
799.3'2--dc20                                                    96-16958
                                                                    CIP

ISBN: 0-87322-854-5

**Developmental Editor:** Julia Anderson;  **Assistant Editor:** Jacqueline Eaton Blakley; **Editorial Assistant:** Coree
Schutter; **Copyeditor:** Heather Stith; **Proofreader:** Sarah Wiseman; **Graphic Designer:** Keith Blomberg; **Graphic
Artists:** Denise Lowry and Kathleen Boudreau Fuoss; **Cover Designer:** Jack Davis; **Photographer (cover):** Wilmer
Zehr—equipment provided by Ridge Runners Archery, Cooks Mills, IL; **Illustrators:** Tim Offenstein, Denise Lowry,
and Pam Shaver; **Printer:** United Graphics

Instructional Designer for the Steps to Success Activity Series: Joan N. Vickers, EdD, University of Calgary, Calgary,
Alberta, Canada

Human Kinetics books are available at special discounts for bulk purchase.  Special editions or book excerpts can
also be created to specification.  For details, contact the Special Sales Manager at Human Kinetics.

Printed in the United States of America        10  9  8

**Human Kinetics**
Web site: www.HumanKinetics.com

*United States:* Human Kinetics, P.O. Box 5076, Champaign, IL 61825-5076
800-747-4457
e-mail: humank@hkusa.com

*Canada:* Human Kinetics, 475 Devonshire Road, Unit 100, Windsor, ON N8Y 2L5
800-465-7301 (in Canada only)
e-mail: orders@hkcanada.com

*Europe:* Human Kinetics, 107 Bradford Road, Stanningley
Leeds LS28  6AT, United Kingdom
+44 (0) 113 255 5665
e-mail: hk@hkeurope.com

*Australia:* Human Kinetics, 57A Price Avenue, Lower Mitcham, South Australia 5062
08  8277 1555
e-mail: liahka@senet.com.au

*New Zealand:* Human Kinetics, P.O. Box 105-231, Auckland Central
09-523-3462
e-mail: hkp@ihug.co.nz

# Contents

# PREFACE

When we started shooting archery, we were drawn by the challenge of trying to shoot an arrow into the bull's-eye. Each shot that hit the bull's-eye would encourage us to keep trying. At first, hitting a bull's-eye was one of those fundamental tests of skill, like trying to throw a ball a certain distance or complete a race in a certain amount of time. Archery looked easy compared to many of the other sports we had tried. The more we were around archers, though, the more we could see that the challenge wasn't just to hit the bull's-eye once in a while. Rather, the challenge was to hit the bull's-eye with every shot. This challenge was not so easily met.

We have found many ways of enjoying archery. We started shooting archery indoors at 20 yards. Just when we could shoot a good percentage of arrows into the bull's-eye, we discovered outdoor shooting and found it wasn't so easy—especially from 65 yards in the wind! Simulated bowhunting tournaments provided the challenge of shooting from unmarked distances. We also found a source of pleasure and pride in maintaining and adjusting our own equipment. There always seems to be something new and challenging about archery, despite its seemingly simple goal of hitting your mark.

Hearing from the many shooters who discovered this same challenge through the first edition of *Archery: Steps to Success* has been rewarding and exciting. We are teachers by instinct, desire, and profession, and we enjoy sharing this sport with others. Between us, we have taught archers of all ages. Our experience undoubtedly benefits our students. This text gives us the opportunity to reach many more novice archers than we could reach in person.

We have seen many archers start off on the wrong foot for various reasons. In some cases, they had no one to systematically teach them the basics. In other cases, they had no one to identify and correct their errors before they became habit, or they were handed ill-fitting equipment or too many accessories at once. Archery is one of those sports in which novices can experience early success even with technique flaws. This short-term success usually gives way to frustration as the effects of technique flaws become more noticeable.

In this second edition of *Archery: Steps to Success,* we strengthen the emphasis on sound, basic technique. Regardless of whether you have picked up this book because you are interested in target archery or bowhunting, shooting a traditional recurve bow or a compound bow, you will benefit from sound fundamentals. From this starting point, you can refine your technique and vary it for specific forms of archery or types of equipment.

The first eight steps of this text take you from your very first shot to a level of technique and performance you can then adapt to your particular interest, target shooting or bowhunting. These interests are each addressed in the final two steps. The Keys to Success and Success Stoppers in each chapter or step of this text give you the means to monitor your adherence to good technique on your own. If you are learning archery on your own or have solo practice sessions between classes, this text shows you how to analyze your shooting and make corrections to put you back on the track to success.

The drills and practice activities included in this text are somewhat unique for an archery book. Because archery practice traditionally consists of merely shooting, many novice archers find practice a chore. The drills provided in each step of this book should keep your practice sessions focused and provide some variety for your shooting. They also enable you to break down your shooting technique to focus on a particular aspect of form or equipment. So, rather than attempting to monitor all of your positions and movements on every shot, you can practice one thing at a time.

We arrived at the second edition of this text through the help of many others. First, we would like to acknowledge Joan Garrison, a master teacher from whom Kathie Haywood took her undergraduate archery class. It is ideal to have a good model for archery instruction from the start. Second, we would like to thank Earl Hoyt, Jr., master bowyer, for his willingness to share his vast knowledge of archery with us. We'd like to acknowledge, too, the influence of Al Henderson's writings. Sometimes they were the only source we could find on an aspect of shooting. Thanks to Cynthia Haywood Kerkemeyer for help with illustrations and to the many archers and teachers who passed along suggestions for the second edition.

# THE STEPS TO SUCCESS STAIRCASE

Get ready to climb a staircase—one that will lead you to become an accomplished archer. You cannot leap to the top; you get there by climbing one step at a time.

Each of the 10 steps you will take is an easy transition from the one before. The first few steps of the staircase provide a solid foundation of basic skills and concepts. As you progress, you will learn how to aim with a bowsight, analyze and improve your performance, and develop positive mental skills. As you near the top of the staircase, you will become more confident in your ability to tune your own equipment, compete in tournaments, and if you choose, bowhunt.

Familiarize yourself with this section as well as "The Sport of Archery" and "Equipment and Accessories" sections for an orientation and in order to understand how to set up your practice sessions around the steps. Follow the same sequence each step (chapter) of the way:

1. Read the explanations of what is covered in the step, why the step is important, and how to execute or perform the step's focus, which may be basic skills, concepts, tactics, or a combination of the three.
2. Follow the numbered illustrations showing exactly how to position your body to execute each shot successfully. The three general parts to shooting in any situation are stance, draw and aim, and follow-through.
3. Look over the common errors that may occur and the recommendations for how to correct them.
4. Read the directions and the Success Goal for each drill. The drills help you improve your skills through repetition and purposeful practice. Practice accordingly and record your scores. Compare your score with the Success Goal for the drill. You need to meet the Success Goal of each drill before moving on to practice the next one because the drills are arranged in an easy-to-difficult progression. This sequence is designed specifically to help you achieve continual success.
5. As soon as you can reach all the Success Goals for one step, you are ready for a qualified observer, such as your teacher, coach, or trained partner, to evaluate your basic skill technique against the Keys to Success Checklist. This qualitative or subjective evaluation of your basic technique or form is useful because using correct form can enhance your performance.
6. Repeat these procedures for each of the 10 Steps to Success. Then rate yourself according to the directions in the "Rating Your Progress" section.

Good luck on your step-by-step journey to developing your archery skills, building confidence, experiencing success, and having fun!

# THE SPORT OF ARCHERY

When you pick up a bow to shoot your first arrow, you are partaking in an activity dating back at least 20 thousand years. The bow and arrow are pictured in drawings that old on a cave wall in Spain's Valltorta Gorge.

The bow and arrow were once critical to humankind's survival. The bow allowed humans to become proficient hunters. Prey provided various raw materials, such as hide, bone, and sinew, for tools, shelter, and clothing and added more protein to the diet. Hunting with a bow was safer than other methods because prey could be shot from a distance. Early bow designs reflected the materials available in the geographic region, the tools available for craftsmen, and the ways in which the bow was used. For example, short bows were easier to handle from horseback or a chariot, and long bows were better for shooting distant targets from a fortified encampment.

Empires rose and fell through the use of the bow and arrow as weapons. The ancient Egyptians first established the bow as a primary weapon of war around 3500 B.C. They made bows almost as tall as themselves and arrowheads of flint and bronze. Around 1800 B.C., the Assyrians introduced a new bow design: a short composite bow of leather, horn, and wood with a recurve shape. It was more powerful than the longbow used by the Egyptians and could be handled easily on horseback. This bow gave the Assyrians an edge in battle over their Middle-Eastern rivals. The Hittites also used the short recurve bow in mobile warfare by shooting from the light, fast chariots they developed around 1200 B.C.

Middle-Eastern superiority in archery continued for centuries as the peoples of this area successfully fought Europeans. For example, the Romans, although known as mighty soldiers, used an inefficient draw to the chest in shooting the bow and were outclassed as archers by the third-century Parthians of Asia. The Mongols conquered much of Europe, and the Turks threw back the Crusaders, in part because of their superior recurve bows and better shooting technique.

In the 11th century, the Normans developed a longbow that they used along with superior battle strategy to defeat the English at the Battle of Hastings in 1066 A.D. Thereafter, the English adopted the longbow as their major weapon and abandoned their Saxon-style bow, which was weaker and less accurate. Many ballads of the 13th and 14th centuries, such as the tales of Robin Hood, attest to the archery skill that the English developed with the longbow.

Although the value of the bow as a war weapon declined swiftly after the invention of firearms in the 16th century, the fun and challenge of archery guaranteed its continued existence as a sport. King Henry VIII promoted archery as a sport in England by directing Sir Christopher Morris to establish an archery society, the Guild of St. George, in 1537. Roger Ascham published the book *Toxophilus* in 1545 to preserve much of the archery knowledge of the time and to maintain interest in archery among the English. Archery societies were founded throughout the 1600s, and the tournaments they held firmly established archery as a competitive sport. The Ancient Scorton Silver Arrow Contest was first held in 1673 in Yorkshire, England, and continues to be held today. Women joined the men in competition and were first admitted to an archery society in 1787.

On the North American continent, Indians relied on the bow and arrow for hunting. Indian bows, however, were short and weak; the hunter had to get close to prey to be successful. Some Indian tribes hunted from horseback, riding up next to game; others hid in forested areas, waiting for game to come in range. European settlers brought their well-developed knowledge of bowmaking from their native countries and kept interest in target archery alive in North America. The first archery club on the continent, the United Bowmen of Philadelphia, was established in 1828.

Oddly, the Civil War spurred greater interest in archery in the United States. When the war ended, the victorious Union prohibited former Confederate soldiers from using firearms. Two veteran brothers, Will and Maurice Thompson, learned archery with the help of Florida Indians. Maurice wrote a book, *The Witchery of Archery*, that helped spread interest in archery across the country. By 1879, the National Archery Association was founded and began holding national tournaments. Enthusiasm for field archery (a target archery competition that simulates hunting) and bowhunting itself led to establishment of the National Field Archery Association in 1939.

Archery first became an official Olympic event at the Paris Olympics in 1900, an appropriate sanctioning as the mythical founder of the ancient Olympics was Hercules, an archer. Archery was an event at the 1904 St. Louis Olympics and the 1908 Olympics in England, but it did not reappear until 1920 when the Olympics were held in Belgium. Archery failed to appear in any of the Olympic games held over the next 52 years.

The problem with early archery competition was the lack of a universal set of rules. The host country had usually held the archery contest most popular in that country. If archery was not popular in the host country, the event was not even held during athletic meets. To better organize competitive archery, Polish archers worked to establish an international governing body during the 1930s. As a result, the Federation Internationale de Tir A L'Arc, known by its acronym FITA, was founded. FITA set up universal rules and designated particular rounds that would be shot in international competitions, including the Olympics. As a result, international competition grew and gained so much momentum in succeeding decades that archery was readopted for the 1972 Olympic games.

Technical advances in bow and arrow design and the availability of new materials have increased shooting accuracy and, consequently, interest in archery. Two developments have had particular impact. In 1946, Doug Easton developed a process for manufacturing aluminum arrow shafts. The uniformity of aluminum arrows in weight and spine (stiffness) greatly increased the accuracy and enjoyment of shooting for many. Then in 1966, H.W. Allen invented the compound bow in Missouri. The compound bow uses eccentric (off-center axle) pulleys or cams that are mounted in the tips of the bow limbs to reduce the holding weight of the bow for a given draw weight. These types of bows are popular in North America for target and field archery, as well as bowhunting.

Recently, new materials such as carbon have led to the design of lighter and therefore faster arrows, more consistent performance of bow limbs, and more flexibility to interchange parts and accessories. New archers today can shoot with great accuracy with this modern equipment.

## Archery Today

Archery is enjoyed today by thousands of people all over the world. One of the reasons for its popularity is that there are many ways to enjoy archery, including target shooting and bowhunting. Archery can be shot by men and women, children and older adults, and those with and without disabilities (see figure 1).

**Figure 1**   Archery is popular with people of all ages and ability levels.

### Target Archery

Target archery has been popular since the days of King Henry VIII of England. The challenge of hitting your mark is timeless. Today, many archers enjoy shooting recurve bows by using their fingers to release the string. In the United States, the National Archery Association traditionally sponsors competition for archers using this equipment.

The National Field Archery Association and the Professional Archers Association promote competition with the compound bow in the United States. Bowsights with magnification and illumination are permitted in these competitions. There is also an equipment class that allows archers to use a mechanical triggering device to hold and release the string (see figure 2). Archers in this classification may well shoot a perfect score in a round, with all arrows landing in a tie-breaking X-ring within the bull's-eye.

Field archery associations usually add equipment classifications for target competition that require equipment similar to that used for hunting. The number of fixed sight pins, and therefore, sight settings is limited, as are aiming aids. The arrows must be of the type used for hunting, with a target tip installed rather than a broadhead, though.

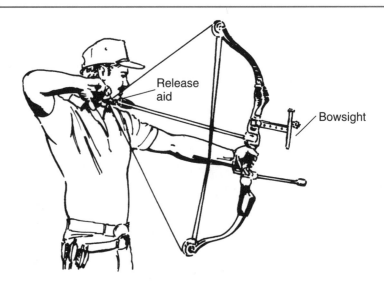

Release aid

Bowsight

**Figure 2** Special bowsight and release aid.

## Other Types of Archery

Bowhunting is a popular activity today. Bowhunters enjoy the challenge of taking game as they help to control the size of game populations whose natural predators have dwindled. The amount of game taken during a season is usually regulated. The majority of bowhunters now use compound bows, making bowhunting more humane because a kill is more likely than a wound with the increased arrow speed and potential for heavier draw weight that the compound bow affords. The compound bow also allows smaller persons to hunt with the necessary bow draw weight (see figure 3).

**Figure 3** Compound bows allow smaller persons to hunt with the necessary draw weight.

Bowhunting has become so popular that bowhunters often hold competitive rounds in the off season. Silhouette or three-dimensional (3-D) foam targets are placed in wooded areas at unmarked distances. Equipment is often limited to that used for hunting. The Archery Shooters Association, International Bowhunting Organization of the U.S., and the Professional Bowhunters Society all sponsor such competitions in the United States.

Bowfishing is another way to enjoy archery. Fish are shot from a boat or canoe with an arrow attached to fishing line. A special reel is mounted onto the face of the bow. The fish taken are often carp, gar, buffalo, suckers, redhorse, stingray, and skates. Most effective shots are taken through a depth of four feet or less because the water quickly slows an arrow.

Flight shooting is yet another type of archery enjoyed in some parts of North America. Arrows are shot for distance. Special bows and arrows are designed for just this purpose. Today's flight bows shoot over 900 yards (see figure 4).

**Figure 4** A flight bow.

Novelty shoots are occasionally held for enjoyment and variety. These shoots sometimes take the form of clout shooting, wherein a 48-foot target is laid on the ground and shot at from 140 to 180 yards. Archery golf, which is shot similar to golf, involves shooting a flight arrow, an approach arrow, and a putting arrow at a four-inch ball. In roving, archers in a small group take turns choosing and then shooting at a target to see who can come the closest.

Some parts of North America also have crossbow competitions. Technical advances in crossbow design and materials have made crossbows very accurate. Today's shooters aim for 60-centimeter target faces from distances as great as 65 meters.

Soon, technological advances will allow archers to shoot at virtual images generated by computer systems. The number and type of "games" created by such systems could be limitless. No matter which form of archery or what type of equipment you come to enjoy, the same basic form and shot-to-shot consistency leads to shooting accuracy. The equipment and your physical and mental skills must come together to produce the perfect shot.

## Shooting Target Archery

Competitive target archery can be shot in many different types of rounds or contests, unlike most sports where a single set of rules governs play. For example, indoor contests are usually shot at a single, short (20 yards or meters) distance at a single size target. Each outdoor contest, though, is usually shot at various distances with targets of variable size, depending on the distance. Some rounds call for just 1 shooting distance, others 3 or 4, and still others require 10 or more. The number of arrows shot in a round also varies. Indoors, 30, 45, or 60 shots is typical, but 56 to 144 shots per round is common outdoors. Tournaments can consist of one or more rounds. Sometimes different types of rounds are shot within the same tournament.

Unless the round simulates hunting, a target of concentric circles is used, and the closer an arrow lands to the center of the target, the more points are awarded. One thing is typical of all the various rounds. The score of individual arrows is totaled, and the archer with the highest point total wins the contest. In recent years, some archery tournaments have used head-to-head competition, sometimes after a traditional round to establish seedings, with the winner advancing until a single archer is declared champion. These formats are particularly exciting for spectators.

Competitive target archery is also shot with a variety of bows, although archers are often separated into classes within a tournament or into different tournaments based on their equipment. The traditional recurve bow consists of a handle riser section made of metal, often magnesium. The bow limbs are usually composites of wood and fiberglass, plastic, or carbon. An adjustable sight is mounted on the bow, as are one or more rods called stabilizers, which reduce the tendency of the bow to turn on its long axis upon release of the arrow (see figure 5).

The compound bow also has a metal handle riser, but its limbs might be composite or solid fiberglass. Eccentric pulleys or cams are mounted on the limb tips. Steel cables are attached to the pulleys, and the bowstring, in turn, is attached to the cables. A compound bow can also be equipped with adjustable sights and stabilizers.

The target arrow is usually made of aluminum, carbon, or a combination of the two. It is equipped with a steel tip that is bullet-shaped. Real feathers or plastic vanes are attached to the back end of the arrow. In modern target archery, all of an archer's arrows should be identical in size, weight, and length.

Competitive target archery is shot with sophisticated equipment. Yet the variability of a novice's accuracy is often due more to basic form and technique than to equipment. A simple, one-piece, traditional bow and wood or fiberglass arrows are sufficient for learning the basic techniques of archery.

Sight

■ **Figure 5**   A bow with an adjustable sight.

## Shooting Rules

The various archery associations, kinds of equipment, and types of rounds lead to variations in archery rules. You need to be familiar with the specific set of rules that govern any class, range, or contest in which you participate. Many of the rules are similar, however, and the following set of common archery rules for shooting and scoring will suffice for your early experiences in archery. Later in this book, you must learn a set of safety rules.

1. If you shoot with a class or at an indoor range, the shooting distance will be specified. If there is a shooting line, stand with one foot on each side of the line when shooting.
2. There will be an established number of arrows to be shot at one time. This number is called an end. It is discourteous to shoot more than this number of arrows.
3. If you are shooting with a group, someone may be assigned to control shooting with a whistle: One blast signals the beginning of shooting; two blasts indicate archers may go forward to the target to score (see figure 6) and collect arrows; four or more blasts indicate that all shooting must immediately cease. If no one is controlling the shooting, be sure to wait until all archers have finished shooting before you go forward to retrieve your arrows.
4. Archery targets can be of various types, depending on the round shot. Arrows in the official five-colored, 10 scoring ring target face count as follows from the center out: 10 points, 9 points, 8 points, 7 points, 6 points, 5 points, 4 points, 3 points, 2 points, and 1 point.

5. If an arrow touches two scoring areas on the target face, the higher score counts.
6. If an arrow drops from the bow as you are nocking, drawing, or letting down, you can reshoot that arrow provided that you can retrieve it without leaving the shooting line. If you cannot reach it, the arrow is considered shot. You can retrieve it when the signal to retrieve arrows is given. It is scored as 0 points.
7. If you shoot at an outdoor range, shoot from the same distance as any other archers already shooting when you arrive, unless you leave an open target between your target and those of the other archers by doing so.

**Figure 6** Archers advancing to retrieve their arrows after the two-blast signal.

## Preparing Your Body for Success

Archery is not as vigorous as most other sports, but archers must exert force using the same back and arm muscles on every shot. Strength is an obvious advantage in shooting. Muscle balance and flexibility are advantages as well. Archers should use regular strength and flexibility exercise to offset overuse imbalances and injuries from the repetitive motions of the shot.

Try to strengthen your muscles, especially the arm, shoulder, and trunk muscles, through a resistance (weight) training program. Ideally, you should do your routine three times a week. Increased strength allows you to shoot a bow of higher poundage that shoots arrows in a flatter trajectory. Increased muscle endurance allows you to shoot long practice sessions without a breakdown in technique as you tire. Make sure your resistance training routine is a balanced one that covers all the upper body muscle groups, both sides of the body, and both muscle groups for movement in a given plane (flexors and extensors). Your emphasis might be on the upper body, but remember that strong legs provide a solid foundation for your shot.

An ideal way to maintain flexibility and muscle balance, and to prepare for shooting, is to develop a preshooting stretching routine. A few minutes of vigorous activity, such as jogging, rope jumping, walking, or jumping jacks, warms the muscles before you stretch. Try to do a stretch for each plane and direction of movement in the upper body joints. Stretch slowly into position and hold for 10 seconds. Repeat each stretch three to six times. Avoid bouncing or forceful twisting motions. Breathe normally. After stretching, draw your bow several times without shooting (ease the string back; do not release it without an arrow in place).

If time permits, you should repeat your stretching routine after shooting, too. This is a good time to work on increasing your range of motion because the exercise of shooting has increased blood flow to the muscles.

# EQUIPMENT AND ACCESSORIES

Equipment is important to your success in archery. Quality equipment fit to your size, strength, and interests can bring you success for many years. Quality equipment is also expensive. The more knowledgeable you are about archery tackle, or equipment, the better you can choose the type of equipment to use and the more assured you can be that the equipment you choose matches your size and strength.

In this section, you will learn about basic archery equipment and accessories, including terms for various pieces of equipment and the advantages and disadvantages of each type of equipment. Information about advanced accessories is also included. You can read about advanced accessories now or come back to this material later.

## Choosing a Bow

Two types of bows are commonly in use today. One type uses the bow limbs to store the energy to propel the arrow. You will probably encounter two variations of this type in an instructional setting. One variation is a straight-limb bow made of solid fiberglass (see

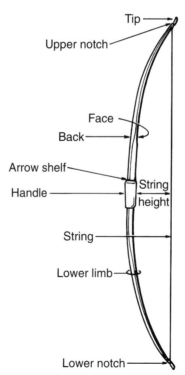

**Figure 7** A straight-limb fiberglass bow.

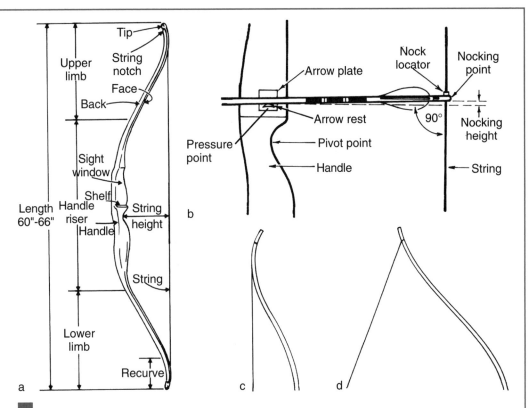

**Figure 8** Various views of a recurve bow: (a) bow with major parts labeled; (b) close-up of arrow rest and nocking point area; (c) bow limb in relaxed position; (d) bow limb in drawn position.

figure 7), and the other is a recurve bow made of laminations of wood and fiberglass (see figure 8a-d). Each variation has its advantages and disadvantages (see table 1). The other type of bow stores energy in an off-center pulley or cam and is known as a compound bow.

## Straight-Limb Fiberglass Bows

The straight-limb fiberglass bow is inexpensive, and both right-handed and left-handed shooters can use the same bow. However, the straight-limb bow design does not provide very much leverage when an archer bends the limbs by pulling back the bowstring. Also, the arrow sits to the right or left of center, and the archer must compensate for this setup when aiming. Straight-limb bows are adequate for beginners because the initial emphasis should be on learning proper shooting form. Serious archers rarely use straight-limb bows, however.

## Recurve Bow

The recurve bow design is more efficient than the straight-limb bow design. A recurve bow in its relaxed position has limb tips that are bent back, away from the archer. The bowstring lies across two to three inches of the limb. When the bowstring is drawn back, the curves straighten to provide leverage. When the string is released, the curves return to their C shape. This series of actions imparts more arrow speed than a straight limb. The length of the limbs is fitted for an archer's size to maximize the leverage that the limbs provide. This quality is called cast. The terms used to describe the various parts of both straight-limb and recurve bows are given in figures 7 and 8. Note that the back of a bow's limbs is the surface facing away from the archer.

| Table 1   Advantages and Disadvantages of Various Bows | | |
|---|---|---|
| **Type of bow** | **Advantages** | **Disadvantages** |
| **Straight-limb fiberglass** | Inexpensive | Little cast |
| | Can be fitted for right-handers or left-handers | Not center-shot |
| **Recurve** | Greater cast | Shooting for distance requires high draw weight |
| | Greater arrow speed | |
| | Interchangeable limbs if take-down style | |
| **Compound** | Holding weight is less than draw weight | Must be fitted for archer's draw length |
| | Potentially faster arrow speed | |

## Compound Bows

Compound bows are characterized by an off-center, or eccentric, pulley or cam mounted on each limb tip (see figure 9). The energy required to rotate the part of the pulley with the long radius is greater than the energy required to rotate the part with the short radius. The pulleys are mounted so that the energy required to pull back the bowstring is the greatest at mid-draw and the smallest at full draw when the archer is holding to aim. When the archer releases the bowstring, this situation is reversed, and the energy applied to the

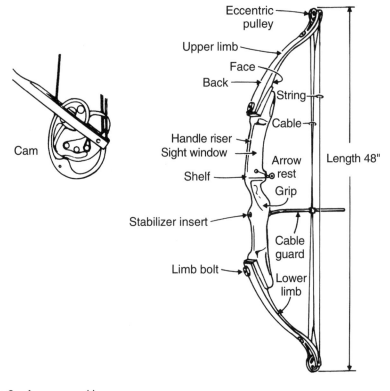

**Figure 9**  A compound bow.

arrow is increased. For example, an archer with a 40-pound compound bow of 50 percent let-off or reduction holds only 20 pounds of resistance at full draw. Forty pounds of thrust, however, are imparted to the arrow.

### Which Type of Bow Is Right for You?

Both modern recurve and compound bows make it possible to shoot with great precision. Your decision about which to use depends in part on whether you would like to enter competitive archery or bowhunting events. Because compound bows allow archers the advantage of shooting arrows with many more pounds of thrust than is required to aim the arrows, separate competitive divisions are usually held for compound and recurve bow shooters. If your interest is target archery, visit local archery clubs and ranges. Find out if the competitive events in your geographical location include both divisions. This information might influence your decision.

Because most hunters use compound bows, this type of bow typically dominates competitive hunting events. If your goal is primarily hunting, you probably want to choose a compound bow that is camouflaged rather than brightly colored. If you decide you want to use a compound bow, remember you can still learn to shoot with a recurve bow. You can better obtain a precision fit in a compound bow once you have increased your strength and solidified your shooting form.

## Choosing Arrows

Five types of arrows are commonly found on the market today: wood, fiberglass, aluminum, carbon, and aluminum-carbon. Just like bows, the various types of arrows have advantages and disadvantages (see table 2). The basic terminology used to describe the parts of an arrow is the same for each type and is given in figure 10.

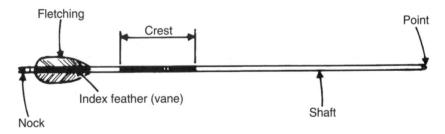

**Figure 10** Parts of a target arrow.

Wood arrows are acceptable for beginning archers because they are inexpensive, but these arrows are not very durable and they easily warp. Because of differences in the pieces of wood used to make arrows, they cannot be closely matched. As a result, an archer might find variation in arrow flight from arrow to arrow.

Fiberglass arrows are more durable than wood arrows, and fiberglass arrows can also be sized to fit archers of varying arm length and strength. Fiberglass arrows of a given size can be manufactured more consistently than wood. However, fiberglass arrows break easily.

Aluminum arrows can be manufactured such that arrows of a given size meet the same specifications and consequently are more accurate than wood or fiberglass. Archers can therefore purchase additional arrows to match their originals at any time. Aluminum arrows

| Table 2 | Advantages and Disadvantages of Various Arrows | | |
|---------|------------------------------------------------|--|--|
| **Type of arrow** | | Advantages | Disadvantages |
| **Wood** | | Inexpensive | Cannot be matched to each other |
| | | | Not readily matched to archer's draw length and weight |
| **Fiberglass** | | Can be sized to draw length and weight | Break easily |
| | | Can be better matched than wood | |
| **Aluminum** | | Can be precisely manufactured | Expensive |
| | | Wide range of sizes available | |
| | | Durable | |
| | | Arrow tips can be interchanged | |
| **Carbon and aluminum-carbon** | | Fast | Very expensive |
| | | | Carbon layer breaks down if struck |

are manufactured in a wide variety of sizes and in different qualities of aluminum alloy. Because you can straighten bent arrows and easily replace damaged arrow points, you can maintain a good set of aluminum arrows for quite some time. Although these arrows are more expensive, their consistency and durability make them the arrow of choice.

Aluminum-carbon arrows are made of an aluminum core wrapped with carbon. Carbon and aluminum-carbon arrows are smaller and lighter than pure aluminum arrows. However, carbon and aluminum-carbon arrows are extremely expensive and are typically used by archers shooting long distances outdoors. These arrows tend to be impractical for archers who tightly pack their arrows in a target, which is typical when shooting short distances, because the carbon wrapping breaks down when it is struck.

## Choosing Accessories That Make Shooting More Comfortable

Several accessories make shooting comfortable and more accurate. One is an arm guard worn on the forearm of the hand holding the bow (see figure 11). This guard provides protection from the bowstring in case the bowstring slaps the forearm upon the bowstring's release. This guard also minimizes the effect on the bowstring and arrow flight should such contact occur.

Another accessory is a finger tab worn over the fingers that hold the bowstring (see figure 12). This tab both protects the fingers and improves the smoothness of the bowstring's release.

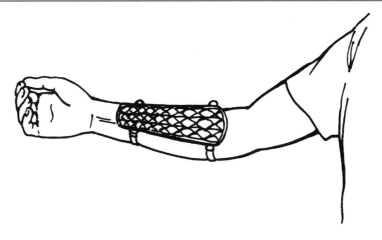

■ **Figure 11**   The arm guard is worn over the inside of the bow arm (left-handed shooter).

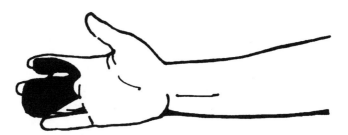

■ **Figure 12**   The finger tab covers the pads of the fingers that hook the bowstring.

A quiver is a handy accessory for holding or carrying arrows. It also minimizes injuries by keeping sharp arrow tips contained. Quivers come in a variety of styles (see figure 13a-c). Most archers use a belt quiver. If you're shooting outdoors, a ground quiver that is stuck into or set on the ground might be convenient to use.

## Choosing Basic Accessories That Increase Accuracy

An arrow rest is an important accessory. It is mounted on the bow above the bow shelf (see figure 14a and b). You place the arrow on the arrow rest and keep the arrow there until you shoot it. The advantage of shooting an arrow off an arrow rest over shooting an arrow off the bow shelf is that the arrow rest allows the fletching on an arrow to clear the bow more smoothly on the arrow's flight toward the target. This advantage results in smoother arrow flight and consequently more accurate shooting. Arrow rests vary in type and cost. The most expensive ones are adjustable so that a bow can be precisely tuned for ideal arrow flight. For your initial experience in archery, a simple arrow rest will suffice.

The bowsight is an attachment to the bow that places a marker, or aiming aperture, in the bow window. To aim, you line up the aperture with the bull's-eye rather than look at the relationship between the arrow and bull's-eye. With a bowsight, you can direct an arrow to the same place, horizontally and vertically, on every shot by controlling the elevation and left/right direction of your bow arm. If the arrow is not directed precisely to the bull's-eye, you can adjust the bowsight by an exact amount for subsequent shots.

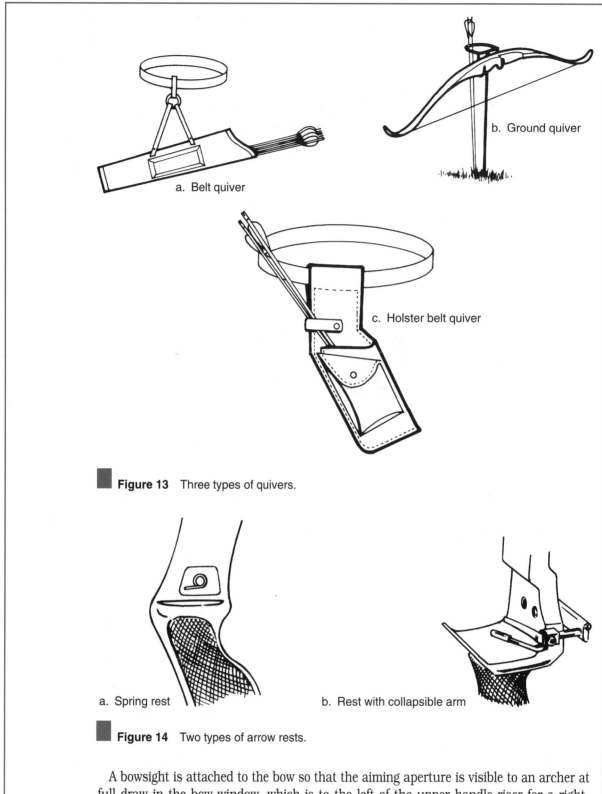

**Figure 13** Three types of quivers.

a. Belt quiver

b. Ground quiver

c. Holster belt quiver

a. Spring rest

b. Rest with collapsible arm

**Figure 14** Two types of arrow rests.

A bowsight is attached to the bow so that the aiming aperture is visible to an archer at full draw in the bow window, which is to the left of the upper handle riser for a right-handed archer. Hunting sights usually have more than one aiming aperture, each of which is set for a different shooting distance. Target sights have one aperture that is repositioned as an archer changes shooting distance.

The aiming aperture should be adjustable, both horizontally and vertically. Having a vertical scale on the bowsight is helpful so that you can record the sight position appropriate for various shooting distances. If the present sight position is directing the arrow slightly high or low for a given shooting distance, a scale also permits you to see exactly how a certain adjustment affects the arrow. Manufactured sights often come with a scale, or you can purchase an adhesive paper scale or even a short metal ruler to mount on the sight.

Target sights can be very simple, inexpensive devices (see figures 15 and 16), or they can be elaborate, precisely made tools that extend from the bow (see figure 17a and b). Simple sights do a good job of directing the arrow as you desire. The difference between sights is typically the ease and accuracy of moving the aiming aperture.

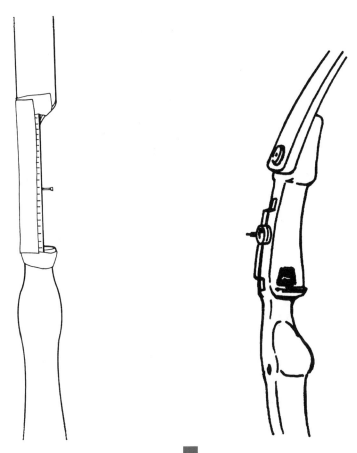

**Figure 15**  A handmade target sight with a pinhead as an aiming aperture.

**Figure 16**  An inexpensive target sight.

Manufactured sights have several types of aiming apertures (see figure 18a and b). Those apertures that are aligned with the middle of the bull's-eye include a simple post with a small round ball on the end, a ring with crosshairs, a ring with a post, and a magnifying lens with a dot in the center. Many archers prefer an open ring. They find it natural to center the bull's-eye inside the ring. Often, the various types of apertures can be interchanged on the more elaborate target sights. You can also purchase aiming apertures with a built-in level. Be aware that rules for competition govern the type of sight and aiming aperture that competitors can use. If you anticipate competing in archery and want to purchase a bowsight, investigate the restrictions that govern your equipment.

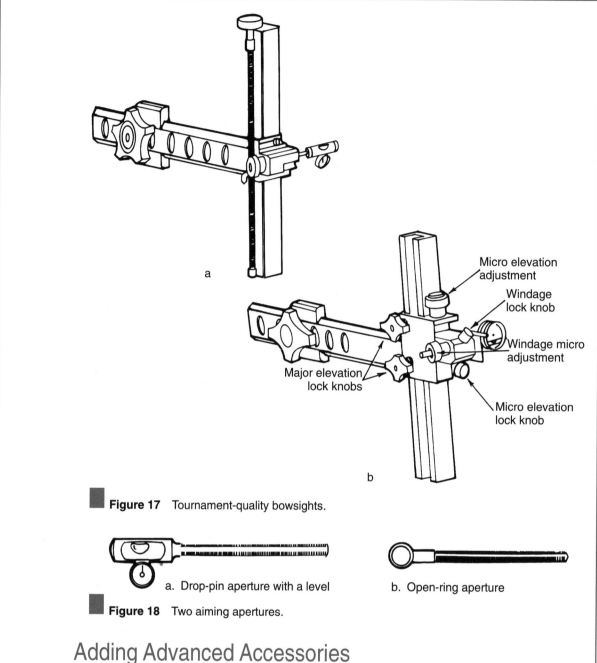

**Figure 17** Tournament-quality bowsights.

a. Drop-pin aperture with a level    b. Open-ring aperture

**Figure 18** Two aiming apertures.

# Adding Advanced Accessories

Several advanced accessories can improve your scoring accuracy even more. These accessories include a bow sling, stabilizers, a kisser button, a peep sight, a draw check, a release aid, and an overdraw.

## Bow Sling

The bow sling is a rope or strap that encircles the hand or fingers and the bow so that the bow will not fall to the ground even if the archer releases the grip on the bow handle (see figure 19). A loose grip on the bow handle is an ideal part of sound shooting technique. A

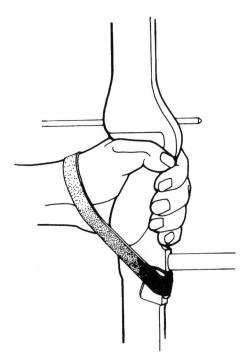

**Figure 19** A bow sling.

bow sling is inexpensive and allows the archer to relax the hand holding the bow without the fear of dropping it.

There are various types of bow slings. Some attach to the bow and the hand is slipped through the strap when the archer takes hold of the bow. Others attach to the thumb and forefinger or to the wrist. The type of sling used is a matter of personal preference. All the types work well and their expense is small in comparison to the improvement in shooting accuracy that comes with a relaxed bow hand.

## Stabilizers

A stabilizer is a metal rod with a weight on its end (see figure 20). High-quality bows come with inserts allowing one or more stabilizers to be attached to the face or back of the bow. A stabilizer is beneficial to shooting accuracy because it reduces the tendency of the bow to turn, or torque, in the bow hand.

When you release the bowstring in shooting an arrow, the arrow pushes against the bow handle. This push causes the bow to turn about its long axis. When you place a weight away from the axis of rotation, you slow and minimize the rotation, which allows the arrow to clear the bow handle before the turning bow handle can seriously affect the arrow. The farther a given weight is from the axis of rotation, or the heavier the weight, the greater is its effect in reducing torque. If you prefer a setup lighter in weight, you can use a lighter weight farther from the axis. If you don't mind the heavy weight, you can use a shorter stabilizer rod. You have many possible combinations of stabilizer length and weight, and you can use more than one stabilizer.

Keep in mind that the stabilizer and weight do add to the weight of the bow, which must be held up and steady throughout the shot. You should develop strength in the bow shoulder by shooting first without a stabilizer, and then adding it when sufficient strength is

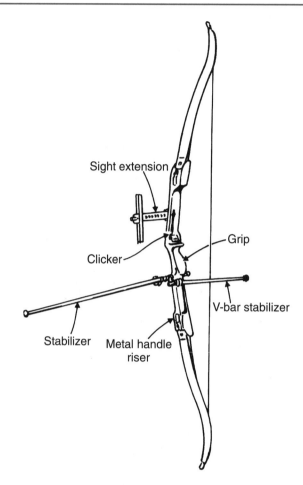

**Figure 20** Bow with a stabilizer attached.

acquired. Follow this same process when increasing the weight at the end of the stabilizer or adding more stabilizers. A reasonable beginning is to add a single stabilizer with a moderate weight to the back of the bow below the grip so that the stabilizer rod extends toward the target. A length of 30 to 33 inches is sufficient.

## Kisser Button

The kisser button is a small, horizontal disc that is attached to the bowstring above the nock locator. The kisser button is set to touch between the lips at full draw (see figure 21). Positioning the hand holding the string, or *anchor*, in the same location on every shot is important. The kisser button aids in maintaining a consistent anchor. Most equipment rules for competition allow a kisser button. Some limit the diameter of the kisser button, and some bowhunter equipment classifications allow the use of a kisser button or peep sight, but not both.

## Peep Sight

The peep sight is a small plastic or metal disc inserted between the strands of the bow-string. It is always used with a bowsight. The archer looks through the peep sight when aiming (see figure 22). Its function is similar to that of a rear sight on a rifle because you are lining up a sight within a sight with the bull's-eye.

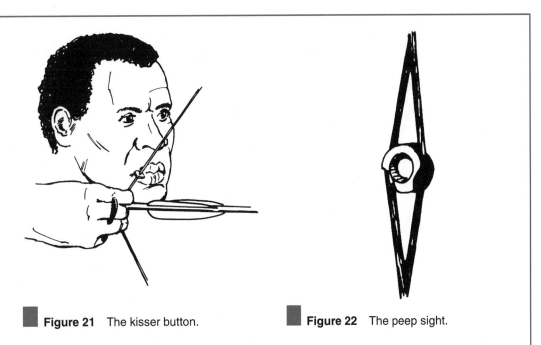

**Figure 21**   The kisser button.

**Figure 22**   The peep sight.

When using a bowsight, you must align the bowstring with the aiming aperture as well as align the aiming aperture with the bull's-eye. Otherwise, the arrow could be directed slightly left or right a varying amount on each shot. The peep sight is placed between the strands of the bowstring, which eliminates the need to align the string and allows for more accurate alignment than is possible when visually aligning the bowstring. The peep sight is not allowed in some equipment classifications for competition. You should wait until you decide what type of archery you enjoy the best and know what the equipment rules are for that type of archery before you install a peep sight.

## Draw Check

A draw check is an accessory that can be helpful to some archers. Even with a solid anchor position, the precise length of the draw may change slightly from shot to shot. A draw check eliminates any variation. There are several types of draw checks; the most common one is a clicker. There is a clicker mounted on the bow pictured in figure 20. A clicker is a single, flat piece of metal under which the arrow is placed when it is nocked. The arrow slides underneath it during the draw. The position of the clicker and length of the arrow are adjusted so that the clicker sits on the taper of the arrow tip when the archer reaches full draw. The archer readies the shot, aims, and then increases the back tension enough that the arrow tip slides from underneath the clicker. The clicker then strikes the bow, and the archer releases upon the sound of the clicker. As a result, the release occurs at exactly the same draw length on every shot.

Many archers use a clicker for reasons other than a check on draw length. For example, some archers tend to release immediately when the sight is aligned with the bull's eye, without allowing the sight to settle. If attempts to overcome this tendency with practice fail, they use clickers to help them release on an auditory signal rather than a visual one. Other archers can have difficulty maintaining back tension throughout their shots and tend to collapse upon release. Clickers force them to increase their back tension until release.

Another type of draw check sometimes used by compound bow archers is cable stoppers. Two blocks are clamped onto the bow's cables. As the bow is drawn and the cables move, the two blocks approach each other until they are flush at full draw. The archer cannot move the bowstring farther back, so the draw length is identical from shot to shot. Through trial and error, the blocks are set in position on the cables to meet when the archer is at full draw.

## Release Aid

Shooting with a release aid is a popular form of archery for hunters and target archers alike. When used properly, the release aid results in more accurate shooting than is possible with the fingers. A single loop of rope or a small metal rod holds the string just below the arrow nock. When the archer triggers the device, the release is cleaner than three, or even two, fingers coming off the string. The string deflection that occurs with a finger release is minimized, so the arrow takes a straighter path to the target. In competitive events, archers using release aids are almost always placed in different divisions than archers releasing the bowstring with their fingers. Usually archers using release aids shoot compound bows.

Release aids are available that are triggered with the index finger, the thumb, or the little finger (see figure 23a-d). Experiment to find the type that works best for you. Some archers believe the models that have the archer pull a trigger back are superior to those that the archer triggers toward the target. Release aid or not, back tension is still a critical ingredient in shooting. Pushing forward on a trigger can result in a slight loss of back tension. Some models also strap around the wrist, allowing the archer to draw with the back muscles while the hand is totally relaxed.

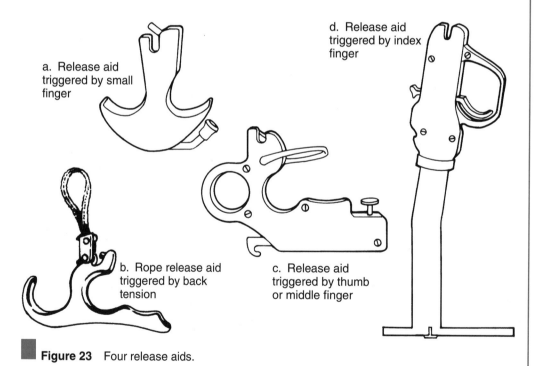

a. Release aid triggered by small finger

b. Rope release aid triggered by back tension

c. Release aid triggered by thumb or middle finger

d. Release aid triggered by index finger

**Figure 23** Four release aids.

## Overdraw

An overdraw is a device that extends the arrow rest toward the archer to permit use of a shorter, and therefore lighter and faster, arrow (see figure 24). Compound bow shooters who use a release aid are the most likely archers to use an overdraw. Care must be taken with an overdraw because the arrow point is drawn behind the bow hand and could injure

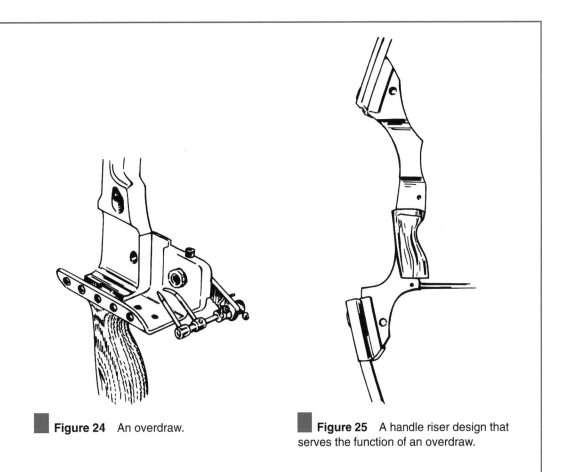

**Figure 24**  An overdraw.

**Figure 25**  A handle riser design that serves the function of an overdraw.

the archer if the arrow slipped off the rest at release. The design of early overdraws made it possible for an arrow to slip off the rest and fall toward the bow arm, but more recent designs incorporate a tray to catch any such arrow. If you decide to try an overdraw, be sure it has such a tray.

Overdraws that extend behind the bow wrist tend to compound the effect of any bow hand and wrist movement upon release, so the overdraw is best used by experienced archers. However, some manufacturers incorporate the benefits of the overdraw into their handle riser design by moving the grip back in relation to the limb attachment location (see figure 25).

*Note:* Shooters who are used to measuring distances in metrics may substitute meters for yards. For example, if the text directs shooting from 10 yards, you may shoot from 10 meters.

# PREPARING TO SHOOT: SELECTING AND SETTING UP YOUR EQUIPMENT

Y ou have probably seen young children trying to hit a ball with a baseball bat or tennis racquet that is too big for them. The problem is obvious. Poorly fitted archery equipment might not be so obvious to the untrained eye, but such equipment causes frustration all the same. Try as you might, you will not have much success with ill-fitted equipment.

Your first step to success in archery is to get equipment matched to your size and strength. The time and effort you put into perfecting your shot technique will yield better scoring results if your equipment is well matched to you and set up properly. Buy the best quality equipment you can afford, but keep in mind that the most expensive equipment in the world will not give you better results if it is not matched to your size and strength. Be wary of using second-hand equipment unless the drills in this step indicate that it is a match to you! Later in this step, you will learn how to set up your bow to shoot. With properly fitted and prepared equipment, you can concentrate on learning good shooting technique because you know you are getting the most from your equipment.

## Why Is Fitting Equipment Important?

In archery, the shooter stores energy in the bow during the drawing of the bowstring. This energy is transferred to the arrow when the archer releases the bowstring. The more energy you can store in the bow, or the higher the draw weight you can pull, the more energy can be transferred to the arrow. You might think it would be worthwhile to contort your body in all sorts of ways in order to use the highest draw weight possible, if it were not for one rather impor-

tant thing—accuracy! In order to shoot accurately, archers must be able to replicate their technique from shot to shot as exactly as possible. To achieve this consistency, you must use a draw weight that is in your comfort range. Draw weight is a function of the physical properties of the bow and the distance of the draw, which is in turn ultimately related to your arm length. For this reason, bows must be fitted to your size and strength.

Later, you will learn more about what happens to an arrow when the bowstring is released. For now, recognize that an arrow can vary in two ways: length and spine (flexibility). For a given bow draw weight and arrow length (both related to your arm length), there is an optimum range of arrow spine. So arrows also must be matched to your size and strength.

## How to Fit Your Bow and Arrows

Determining the right bow for you involves several steps. First, you should decide whether to shoot right- or left-handed. Then, you should determine your draw length and the best bow size. The drills later in this step will take you through these steps.

### Choosing Hand Preference

Choosing whether to shoot right- or left-handed might seem obvious to you. Most right-handers choose to shoot right-handed with their left hand holding the bow and their right hand pulling the bowstring. Certainly right-handers with a dominant right eye should shoot right-handed, and left-handers with a dominant left eye should shoot left-handed.

If you are cross-dominant, which means that your left eye and right hand are dominant or vice versa, you have a choice to make. An archer typically lines up the dominant eye with the target when aiming, so you can shoot on the side of your dominant eye. If you are more comfortable shooting on the side of your dominant hand, you can learn to shoot with your dominant eye closed instead. For example, if you are right-handed and cross-dominant, close your left eye to aim. If you do not, you might line up your left eye with the target and shoot your arrows to the left on some, but not all, of your shots. Drill 1 at the end of this step will help you determine your dominant eye.

## Determining Your Draw Length

You need a draw length measurement to fit both the bow and arrows. Drill 2 at the end of this step will help you determine your draw length. Beginners often obtain a draw length that is slightly shorter than that obtained after they shoot for several weeks. Being new to drawing a bow, they have not yet learned to stretch as far as they should. If you decide to purchase your own equipment after your initial archery lessons, remeasure your draw length.

### Fitting a Recurve Bow

If you are going to be shooting with a recurve bow, you now need to select one that is of proper length and weight. First, determine the bow length ideal for you by using your draw length to find the proper bow length in table 1.1. Next, choose a draw weight. You should start with a light weight that you can pull and easily hold while developing good form.

### Table 1.1 Selection of Bow Length

| Draw length | Bow length |
| --- | --- |
| Under 24 inches | 60-64 inches |
| 25-26 inches | 65-66 inches |
| 27-28 inches | 67-68 inches |
| 29 inches or more | 69-70 inches |

Keep in mind that the draw weight printed on the bow is the draw weight at a standard draw length. Older bows list their draw weight measured at 28 inches from the bowstring at full draw to the back of the bow. Newer bows list their draw weight measured at 26 1/4 inches from the bowstring to the arrow rest. If your draw length is shorter than the standard, the bow limbs will not deflect as far and you will be shooting fewer pounds than the weight stated on the bow. If your draw length is longer than the standard, you will be shooting more pounds than the weight stated. Add two pounds for every inch your draw length is above the standard or subtract two pounds for every inch your draw length is below the standard to estimate the actual bow weight you will be shooting.

Adult archers of average strength typically begin with a bow 20 to 25 pounds in weight. Stronger archers can begin with 25- to 30-pound bows. Lighter bows of 15 to 20 pounds are appropriate for young archers.

### Fitting a Compound Bow

Compound bows must be fitted first for draw weight and draw length, and then for bow length. The holding weight of a compound bow, which is the force that is held at full draw, is a fraction of its peak weight, which is the force that is imparted to the arrow. Obviously, you can select a compound bow of higher draw weight than your recurve bow. You must pull through the peak weight of a compound bow in order to reach the holding weight, so you must have the strength to pull through the peak weight. The archery shop where you purchased your compound bow should have a scale that will measure the bow's peak weight and its holding weight at your draw length.

The size of the eccentric pulley determines the point in the draw where the holding weight is reached. This point is called the valley because it is the point in the draw of the lowest draw weight. Ideally, the valley should correspond to your draw length. Many compound bows today allow an adjustment of approximately three inches in draw length with the same size pulley. This type of pulley makes it easier to fit a compound bow, but your draw length must fall within the specified range for the compound bow, and the bow cables must be placed in the groove of the pulley corresponding to your draw length. If your draw length is over 30 inches, your compound bow should be at least 40 inches long, axle to axle. A length of 44 inches or more is preferable for draw lengths of 33 inches or more. This relationship is usually taken into account by the bow's manufacturer.

## *Choosing Arrows to Fit*

Using arrows of proper length is absolutely critical from a safety perspective. Drawing an arrow past the arrow rest can be dangerous, and this situation is likely to happen with an arrow too short for your draw length. On the other hand, an arrow that is too long does not fly well. As a beginner, you should determine your arrow length by adding at least 3 3/4 inches to your draw length as shown in figure 1.1. When you establish a more consistent form, you can use arrows just 3/4 inch to 1 3/4 inches longer than your draw length.

Arrows also vary in shaft size. The rationale for determining the ideal shaft size is presented in step 8. For now, you can select the size of your arrow shaft from table 1.2 if you are using fiberglass ar-rows or table 8.2 (p. 107) if you are using aluminum arrows. Be sure every arrow in your set is of the same material, shaft size, and length.

| Table 1.2 Shaft Sizes for Fiberglass Arrows | | | | | | | | | |
|---|---|---|---|---|---|---|---|---|---|
| Bow weight at draw length (pounds) | Draw length (inches) | | | | | | | | |
| | 23 | 24 | 25 | 26 | 27 | 28 | 29 | 30 | 31 |
| 20-25 | 0 | 0 | 0 | 1 | 2 | 3 | 4 | 5 | 6 |
| 26-30 | 0 | 0 | 1 | 2 | 3 | 4 | 5 | 6 | 7 |
| 31-35 | 0 | 1 | 2 | 3 | 4 | 5 | 6 | 7 | 8 |
| 36-40 | 1 | 2 | 3 | 4 | 5 | 6 | 7 | 8 | 9 |
| 41-45 | 1 | 2 | 3 | 4 | 5 | 6 | 7 | 8 | 9 |

**FIGURE 1.1** **KEYS TO SUCCESS**

# FITTING ARROWS

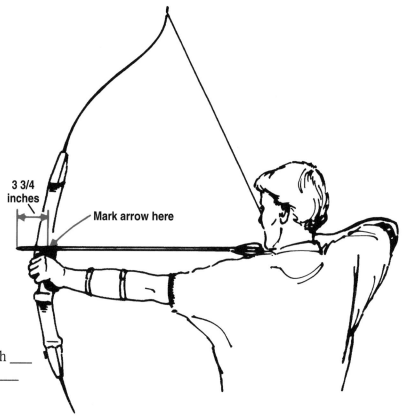

3 3/4 inches

Mark arrow here

1. Add 3 3/4 inches to draw length ___
2. Determine actual draw weight ___
3. Choose shaft size ___

## Fitting Necessary Accessories

The final step in fitting your equipment is to choose an arm guard and finger tab. An arm guard that covers the forearm of your bow arm (the one that holds the bow) should be sufficient. Some archers find that their particular body structure places the upper arm close to the path of the string upon release. They then choose a long style of arm guard that covers both upper arm and forearm.

The finger tab covers the first three fingers of your draw or string hand (the one that pulls the bowstring). Finger tabs come in several sizes. Choose one that covers the fingers when you form a hook to pull the string but that does not have excess leather extending beyond the fingertips. Figure 1.2 shows a properly fitted tab and arm guard.

**FIGURE 1.2**

**KEYS TO SUCCESS**

# FITTING ACCESSORIES

1. Choose arm guard ___
2. Choose finger tab ___

# How to Set Up Your Bow and Accessories

At the very least, you should have a nock locator on your bowstring before you begin shooting and an arrow rest mounted on your bow. You also may want to install a bowsight now, although you could wait until you have made your basic shooting form a habit.

A nock locator guides you in placing your arrows on the bowstring. It guarantees that your arrows will be oriented at the same angle on every shot. Even slight variations in the angle can affect accuracy because a small distance at the tail end of the arrow affects the arrow's trajectory to the target. Nock locators are often a small, C-shaped piece of metal lined with rubber or soft plastic to protect the bowstring. A special pair of pliers is used to tighten the locator on the string. Metal locators are inexpensive and can be repositioned, but some archers simply wrap waxed dental floss around their bowstring to form a nock locator. Most archers place the locator so that the arrow is nocked right below it and the arrow sits very slightly tail high, as shown in figure 1.3a. See drill 5 in this step to learn how to precisely position the nock locator when tuning a bow.

If you are using a fiberglass, straight-limb bow, the bow handle usually serves as arrow rest. Some inexpensive recurve bows also are made with a shelf on which the arrow rests. Most other recurve and compound bows, though, are meant to have an arrow rest installed on them. Some of these bows have a cut-out section in their handle riser. You must purchase an arrow rest and stick it onto the handle riser in the proper location as shown in figure 1.3b. Drill 6 in this step will guide you in positioning such a rest. More expensive recurve and compound bows have a hole in the handle riser that allows the arrow rest to be installed at the proper location. Later, as part of the tuning process, you will learn how to precisely adjust such an arrow rest.

If you have purchased a bowsight, it is probably either a sight mounted flush onto the back of the bow or one extended out from the bow on a bar or bracket. You can install flush-mounted sights on laminated wood and fiberglass bows by drilling two small holes. Be careful when drilling into a laminated wood bow—you don't want to crack the bow or weaken it structurally. You should also use small screws when you install the bowsight. If you are uncomfortable installing your own bowsight, you can have it done at a pro shop, or you can tape your bowsight tightly on your bow.

Extended sights typically come with a mounting bracket that is permanently attached to the side, rather than back, of the bow (see figure 1.3c). The sight and extension bar are clamped onto the bracket for use during shooting sessions and are removed between shooting sessions. The bracket is also mounted onto the bow with screws. Most archers choose the extended sight when using a bow with a metal handle riser that is pretapped for the sight bracket. The metal riser is much stronger than laminated wood and fiberglass and can support the weight of an extended sight. If you are unable to purchase a bowsight but would like to use one, you can easily make a sighting device. Drill 7 in this step will lead you through the process.

If your bow is tapped to accept a stabilizer and you have chosen the type of bow sling that attaches to the bow, install the sling now. Position the sling's bracket over the stabilizer insert and screw in the bolt. You also can attach a stabilizer now, or you can wait until you increase your arm strength and can more easily lift the extra weight and hold it steady.

If you decide to purchase and use a kisser button and/or a peep sight, you can install one or both of these devices now. Drills 8 and 9 lead you through this installation. You may want to wait and install them later, especially if this is your initial shooting experience. Using too many accessories may divert your attention from establishing good form. You also will have a chance later to choose the anchor (string holding) position you prefer. The position of a peep sight and kisser button changes with changes in anchor position. Another reason for waiting is that some competition rules regulate the size of a kisser button, the use of a peep sight, or the use of the two accessories together. You may not want to get used to an accessory that is not allowed in your preferred competition category.

If you choose to shoot a straight-limb or recurve bow, you should unstring it between shooting sessions. If left in the strung position for an extended period of time, a bow's limbs can weaken. In addition, transporting and storing your bow is easier when it is unstrung. You should learn how to string and unstring your straight-limb or recurve bow.

FIGURE
1.3    KEYS TO SUCCESS

# SETTING UP YOUR EQUIPMENT

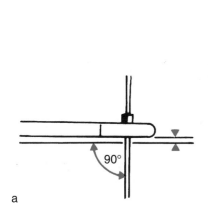

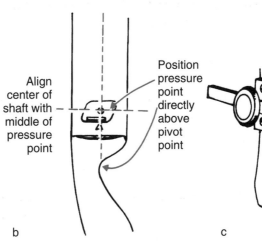

Align center of shaft with middle of pressure point

Position pressure point directly above pivot point

a                                    b                                    c

## The Nock Locator

1. Position bow square on string ___
2. Mark corner of 90-degree angle on the string ___
3. Measure a nock width plus 3/8 inch up from mark ___
4. Position lower edge of nock locator at the point you have determined ___
5. Clamp nock locator ___

## The Arrow Rest

1. Align pressure point over handle pivot point___
2. Attach the rest 5/8 inch above arrow shelf ___

## Other Accessories

1. Attach bowsight ___
2. Attach stabilizers ___
3. Set kisser button ___
4. Clamp kisser button ___
5. Set peep sight ___
6. Tie in peep sight ___

## PREPARING TO SHOOT SUCCESS STOPPERS

Ill-fitted equipment can cause injury and prevent a new archer from learning good technique. A good start to good shooting is obtaining the proper equipment and preparing for shooting. Identify and correct any error in fitting your equipment.

| Error | Correction |
|---|---|
| 1. When trying to determine your dominant eye, your hand comes back to both eyes. | 1. Keep the hole formed by the hands about the size of a nickel. |
| 2. You get a short draw length measurement. | 2. Push the bow arm to the target and pull the string back to the nose when measuring draw length. |
| 3. You strain to draw the string all the way to your nose. | 3. Choose a bow lighter in draw weight, or reduce the draw weight on an adjustable bow. |
| 4. The arrows you chose fall off the back of the arrow rest at full draw. | 4. Make sure you added at least 1 inch, preferably 3 3/4 inches if you are a beginner, to your draw length to arrive at your arrow length. |

## PREPARING TO SHOOT

# DRILLS

### 1. Eye Dominance Drill

You want to know which is your dominant eye in choosing your hand preference for shooting. Place one hand over the other so that a small hole is created between your thumbs and fingers. Extend your arms toward a target. With both eyes open, center the bull's-eye in the opening made by your hands. Slowly bring your arms toward your face while continuing to look at the bull's-eye with both eyes open. When your hands touch your face, the opening should be in front of the dominant eye. An alternative method is to assume the same position, but instead of moving the hands toward the face, keep the arms extended. With both eyes open, center the bull's-eye in the opening, and then close the left eye. If the object remains in view, your right eye is dominant. If not, your left eye is dominant.

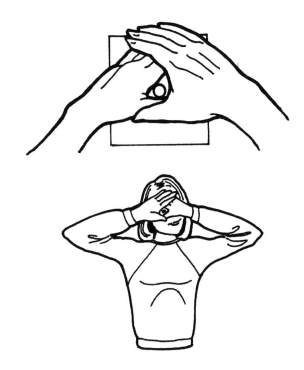

**Success Goal** = Determine your dominant eye ___

**✔Success Check**
• Keep hole about the size of a nickel ___

## 2. Draw Length Drill

To measure draw length, you will need a light-poundage bow and a long arrow. Stand about eight yards from a target. If you are shooting right-handed, hold the bow in your left hand. Hook onto the middle of the bowstring with the first three fingers of your right hand. Raise the bow and pull the string back until the string above your hand touches your nose. Ease the string back. Practice this action several more times, making sure your left arm is fully extended.

Now snap the arrow onto the bowstring beneath the nock locator and place the arrow on the arrow rest of the bow. Pointing the bow toward the target, draw the string back with one finger hooked onto the string above the arrow and the other fingers below the arrow. Have someone mark the arrow directly above the arrow rest. Ease the string back. Measure from the nock slit to the mark. This measurement is your draw length.

**Success Goal** = Determine your draw length ___

**✔Success Check**
• Extend your bow arm to the target ___
• Bring string back to touch nose ___

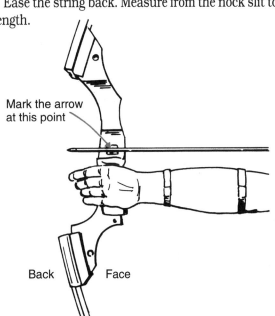

Mark the arrow at this point

Back          Face

### 3. Actual Draw Weight Drill

The poundage given by a recurve bow manufacturer is the poundage at a draw length of 26 1/4 inches. Your draw length is probably different, so your actual draw weight changes by approximately two pounds for every inch of difference.

**Success Goal** = 6 correct estimates of actual draw weight ___

| Case | Draw Length | Draw Weight @ 26 1/4 inches | Actual Draw Weight |
|------|-------------|-----------------------------|--------------------|
| 1 | 24 | 25 | _____ |
| 2 | 25 1/4 | 30 | _____ |
| 3 | 27 3/4 | 30 | _____ |
| 4 | 26 3/4 | 35 | _____ |
| 5 | 28 | 40 | _____ |
| Yours | _____ | _____ | _____ |

**✔ Success Check**

- Add two pounds for every inch over 26 1/4 ___
- Subtract two pounds for every inch under 26 1/4 ___
- Case 1: Actual Draw Weight 20 1/2 pounds
- Case 2: Actual Draw Weight 28 pounds
- Case 3: Actual Draw Weight 33 pounds
- Case 4: Actual Draw Weight 36 pounds
- Case 5: Actual Draw Weight 43 1/2 pounds

### 4. Arrow Selection Drill

To select a fiberglass arrow using table 1.2 (p. 26), find the weight of your bow, adjusted for your draw length, in the first column. Read across to your draw length to determine your ideal shaft size. Select arrows that have this number printed on the sides of their shafts. Directions for finding your ideal aluminum shaft size are given along with table 8.2 (p. 107). Note that this chart requires your arrow length, which is longer than your draw length. The size of an aluminum shaft is printed on its side.

**Success Goal** = 6 correct selections of fiberglass or aluminum arrow shafts ___

| Case | Actual Draw Weight | Draw/Arrow Length | Shaft Size |
|------|--------------------|--------------------|-----------|
| 1 | 25 pounds | 27 inches | _____ |
| 2 | 22 pounds | 26 inches | _____ |
| 3 | 30 pounds | 28 inches | _____ |
| 4 | 40 pounds | 30 inches | _____ |
| 5 | 50 pounds | 31 inches | _____ |
| Yours | _____ | _____ | _____ |

**✔ Success Check**

- Read across to your draw or arrow length ___
- Case 1: Shaft Size #2 (fiberglass); 1616, 1618, 1713, 1714 (aluminum)
- Case 2: Shaft Size #1 (fiberglass); 1516, 1518 (aluminum)
- Case 3: Shaft Size #4 (fiberglass); 1714, 1716, 1813, 1814 (aluminum)
- Case 4: Shaft Size #8 (fiberglass); 1916, 2013, 2014, 1918, 2016, 2114 (aluminum)
- Case 5: Shaft Size #9 (fiberglass); 2018, 2115, 2213, 2117, 2216 (aluminum)

## 5. Nock Locator Setup

The first step in installing a nock locator is marking the point on the bowstring where the bottom of a nocked arrow forms a perfect 90-degree angle with the string. Bow squares are sold for this purpose, but you can substitute a large mechanical drawing triangle or a carpenter's *L*. From this point, measure up the width of your nock plus 3/8 inch. Clamp the nock locator such that its lower edge is positioned where you have measured. If you intend to use an arrow rest, install the rest before you position your nock locator.

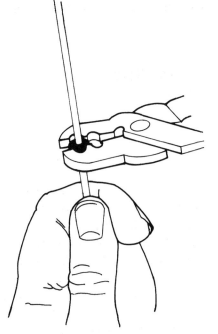

**Success Goal** = Successfully install a nock locator ___

**Success Check**

• Bow square gently contacts arrow rest ___
• Bottom edge of nock locator is a nock's width plus 3/8 inch above 90-degree angle ___

## 6. Arrow Rest Installation

To attach a self-stick arrow rest on a bow not tapped for a cushion plunger, place the bow on a table. Align the pressure point of the rest over the pivot point of the bow handle. Position the rest 5/8 inch above the bow shelf to allow room for the arrow's fletching to clear the shelf upon release. Mark this place with several light pencil marks, peel the paper from the back of the rest, and press it into place.

If you are installing an arrow rest on a bow tapped for a cushion plunger, make sure the cushion plunger is in place first. Then position the rest such that an arrow would contact the rest below the plunger. The center of the arrow also should contact the center of the plunger button.

**Success Goal** = Successfully install an arrow rest ___

**Success Check**

• Align pressure point over pivot point ___
• Place rest 5/8 inch above shelf ___

## 7. Homemade Bowsight Installation

Obtain a five-inch strip of foam, the type sold for insulating window and door jambs, that is 1/2 to 3/4 inch wide. The self-stick variety is easiest to use. Place this strip on the back of your bow even with the sight window (see figure 15, p. 17). Cover it with a piece of tape upon which you can write with a permanent felt marker. Hold a ruler along the tape and place a mark at every half-inch. Number these marks from 1 to approximately 18. Obtain a long straight pin with a ball head and insert this pin into the foam so that it is visible in the sight window. You can move the pin up or down, in or out, to serve as a sight aperture.

**Success Goal** = Make and install a serviceable sight ___

**Success Check**
• Pin head is visible in sight window ___

## 8. Kisser Button Installation

A kisser button is an inexpensive accessory that helps you position your anchor consistently from shot to shot. To position the kisser button properly, slide it onto the bowstring approximately two inches above the nock locator. Draw the string back until the string touches your nose. Feel for the kisser button. Ease the string back. If the kisser button was above or below your lips, adjust it and draw again until the kisser button touches between your lips. You may then want to repeat coming to full draw several times, making sure that you are using the anchor position you want. Once you are satisfied with the kisser button's location, you should mark its place on your bowstring and record its distance from your nock locator. You should clamp down the kisser button so that it will not move. For a nominal cost, you can purchase a small clamp that you can squeeze down over the end of the kisser button with a pair of nocking pliers.

**Success Goal** = Position a kisser button correctly ___

**Success Check**
• Bowstring touches nose ___
• Kisser button touches between lips ___
• Record distance of your kisser button from nock locator: ___

## 9. Peep Sight Installation

A peep sight placed between the strands of the bowstring acts as a rear sight, precisely aligning the bowstring and the tail of the arrow with the bowsight and target. To install a peep sight, you should first place it between the strands of the bowstring above the nock locator at about the height of your aiming eye. Draw to your anchor and note whether you can look through the peep sight to see your bowsight. Ease the bowstring back, and slide the peep sight up or down as needed. You may also have to turn either the peep sight or the bowstring so that the peep hole is fully open to your eye. This is often a process of trial and error. Once you have the peep sight at the correct height, you should mark the bowstring at this location. You might also want to measure and record the distance between the peep sight and your nock locator.

You should tie the peep sight into the string so that it will not move. There are several methods for doing this, but they require practice to complete well, so you may want to take your bow to a pro shop and have an expert tie in your peep sight.

*Success Goal* = Position a peep sight correctly ___

✔*Success Check*
• Bowstring touches nose ___
• Bowsight is visible through center of peep sight ___
• Record distance of peep sight from nock locator: ___

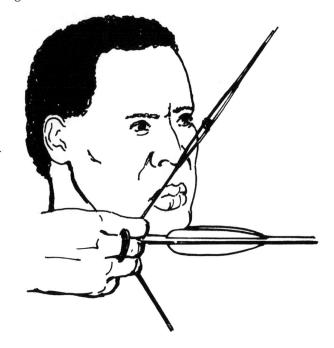

## PREPARING TO SHOOT SUCCESS SUMMARY

You now know how to select a bow that fits you, to select arrows that fit you and are matched to your bow, and to select accessories that fit. You also know how to prepare your bow for shooting. The time spent selecting appropriate equipment and setting it up for shooting is a good investment in your future shooting success and enjoyment. A properly fit bow that matches your personal hand preference, draw length, and strength is more comfortable to shoot than a poorly fitted one. Properly fitted arrows minimize your errors and enable you to have the most scoring success. Some of the steps you completed in fitting and setting up equipment also contribute to safe shooting. Selecting arrows of the proper length makes shooting safe for you, and installing a nock locator makes shooting safer for those around you. Because safety is a great concern in archery, you must now turn your attention to safety, even before you shoot. Ask your teacher, coach, or a friend to evaluate your equipment selection according to the Keys to Success checklists in figures 1.1 through 1.3.

# STEP 2

# SAFETY: BEING CAREFUL AND RESPONSIBLE

When we were kids, the local police department gave a demonstration on the park archery range. A policeman filled a gallon jug with sand and placed a balloon behind it. He fired a handgun into the jug. The sand stopped the bullet. An archer then shot an arrow into the jug. It passed through and popped the balloon. The police made their point to would-be archers: An arrow can be lethal when shot from a bow.

In archery, safety should always come before shooting. In this step, you will learn how to shoot safely to protect both yourself and others. The safety rules are divided into rules that apply before you shoot, rules that pertain to shooting, and rules to keep in mind as your retrieve your arrows.

## Why Be Concerned With Safety?

As you learn about the sport of archery, you must always be aware that you hold a lethal weapon in your hand when you shoot. Before shooting your first arrow, learn safety rules and follow them rigidly. Always keep safety in mind when shooting. Accidents often happen because people are not giving their full attention to the task at hand.

## How to Select and Inspect Equipment for Safety

The first step in safe shooting is choosing equipment that fits properly, as emphasized in step 1. Ill-fitting equipment can be a hazard to you and others around you. Next, inspect your equipment to make sure it is in good working order. This step is particularly important with older equipment, but it should be a regular part of your shooting preparation in any case. Finally, check what you are wearing. Although archery does not require a certain type of clothing, some clothing and accessories can be problematic.

### Equipment Selection

Keep the following points in mind when selecting your equipment.

1. Have an instructor or pro shop employee verify that your arrows are long enough for you. Overdrawing a short arrow is dangerous because the arrow can shatter if it lodges behind the bow; the arrow can even embed itself in your arm (see figure 2.1a).
2. Make sure your arrows are long enough for archers to whom you lend your arrows.
3. Choose a bow draw weight that you can draw easily and hold at least several seconds without tiring.

FIGURE
2.1

## KEYS TO SUCCESS

# EQUIPMENT SELECTION AND INSPECTION

a     ERROR: Overdrawing a short arrow

b     ERROR: Pen in pocket

1. Arrows should be proper length ___
2. Bow weight should be comfortable ___
3. Make sure bowstring is intact ___
4. Do not overdraw arrow ___

5. No cracks should be in bow limbs or arrows ___
6. Wear shoes and close-fitting clothing ___
7. Wear arm guard and finger tab ___
8. Remove jewelry and objects (such as pens in pockets) from clothing ___

### Equipment Inspection

Before shooting, inspect your equipment for the following.

1. Inspect your bowstring. If it is frayed or if any strand of the string is broken, replace the bowstring.

2. Check the serving on your bowstring. If it is unraveling, tie it off, have it re-served, or replace the string.

3. Inspect your bow. If there is a crack in the limbs, do not shoot your bow. Have an instructor or employee at a pro shop inspect it. A cracked bow could break at full draw and cause an injury.

4. If you are shooting with a recurve bow, check the brace height to make sure that it is at least six inches (see figure 2.2). If the brace height is shorter than six inches, the bowstring might slap your wrist.

5. If you are shooting with a compound bow, make sure that the steel cables are routed properly on the pulleys and that the bowstring is securely attached to the cables.

6. Inspect your arrows. Wood arrows with cracks should be broken into two and discarded. Extremely bent aluminum arrows should be straightened before shooting. Each arrow should have a properly installed tip.

7. Inspect your arrows' nocks. Cracked nocks should be removed and replaced immediately because a damaged nock can slip off the string before release.

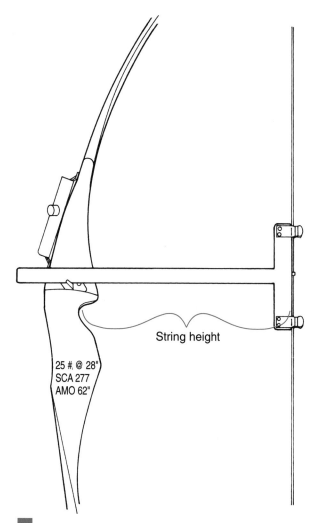

String height

25 # @ 28"
SCA 277
AMO 62"

**Figure 2.2**  A bow square positioned to check the string or brace height.

## *Attire*

Archery requires no particular uniform, but archers avoid clothing that could catch the bowstring. Shoes, armguards, and finger tabs help prevent injuries.

1. When dressing to shoot, avoid baggy shirts, baggy sleeves, and chest pockets with buttons for trim. Remove pens and pencils from shirt pockets (see figure 2.1b). Also, avoid necklaces, dangling earrings, and pins. A bowstring could catch on any of these.
2. If you have long hair, you may want to tie it back so that it does not become caught in the bowstring.
3. Wear shoes when shooting. An arrow dropped on your bare foot or stepped on in the grass could cause an injury otherwise.
4. Wear an arm guard and use a finger tab. They protect you from abrasions and blisters.

## How to Shoot Safely

Most of these safety rules point out in specific ways that a bow is a lethal weapon and that you must be very careful in its use. Dangerous situations must be anticipated.

1. Take your position on the shooting line when instructed to do so, making sure you straddle the line so that you and all shooters are standing in one straight line (see figure 2.3a).
2. Nock your first arrow only after the signal to shoot is given (usually one whistle blast).
3. Point a nocked arrow at the ground until the target area is declared clear and you are ready to draw the bowstring. Even an arrow released from a partially drawn bow can cause serious injury.
4. Nock your arrow only at the nock locator.
5. If shooting on your own, check the target area to make sure that it is clear at least 40 yards behind and 20 yards to each side of the target before each shot.
6. If an arrow falls off the arrow rest, restart the shot rather than attempt to replace the arrow at full draw. Otherwise, you may release the bowstring due to fatigue before getting the arrow into proper position.
7. Learn to shoot without holding the arrow on the bow with your index finger. You could puncture or scratch your finger.
8. If any of your equipment falls forward of the shooting line when you are shooting in a group, rake it toward you with your bow or an arrow (see figure 2.3b) rather than crossing the shooting line to retrieve it.
9. Stop shooting immediately if you hear an emergency signal. Three or more whistle blasts are often used as the emergency signal.
10. Always shoot arrows toward the target; never shoot arrows straight up into the air.

FIGURE 2.3 **KEYS TO SUCCESS**

# SHOOTING SAFETY

a

1. Straddle shooting line ___
2. Point arrow at ground or target ___
3. Make sure area around and behind target is clear ___

b

4. Use bow to rake fallen arrows toward you ___
5. Shoot only at target ___
6. Restart shot if arrow falls off rest ___
7. Stop on emergency signal ___

## How to Safely Retrieve Arrows After Shooting

Amazingly, an archer is more likely to be injured when retrieving and carrying an arrow than when shooting. Not only do arrows have sharp points, they also could cause injury by poking. The broadheads used for hunting deserve the utmost caution. They are razor sharp and can cause severe injury. Adherence to the following rules should help prevent such injuries:

1. Step back from the shooting line when you finish shooting your arrows. If an archer next to you is at full draw, however, it is courteous to remain in place.

2. Place your bow on a bow rack or in a designated area while you retrieve your arrows. Someone could trip over a bow left on the ground or floor.

3. Cross the shooting line to retrieve your arrows only when given the signal to do so (usually two whistle blasts). If no one is providing signals, move forward only after all other archers have stepped back from the shooting line to indicate that they have finished shooting.

4. Walk, rather than run, to the target and approach it with caution (see figure 2.4a). Running or tripping into the nock end of an arrow can cause a serious injury, especially to your eyes.

5. Retrieve low arrows that landed short of the target, in the grass, as soon as possible on the walk to the target. If the fletching is embedded in the grass, pull the arrow forward and out of the grass to keeping from damaging the fletching (see figure 2.4b).

6. Be sure there is no one behind you as you pull your arrows from the target. Place one hand flat

against the target face to prevent it from ripping, and then grasp the arrow shaft close to the target with the other hand (see figure 2.4c). Twist the arrow back and forth to remove it. This twisting keeps the arrow from bending and prevents you from creating a large, forceful backward thrust that could strike someone nearby with the nock end of the arrow.

7. To help prevent eye and head injuries, use caution when retrieving notepads, pens, or other objects below the target.

8. Be careful with arrows because the points are sharp. Carry them in a quiver or with the points in your palm (target points only).

9. When you have to retrieve arrows behind the target, you must be sure no one else will shoot at it. One archer should remain in front of the target while the others look for the lost arrows. If you are shooting alone, leave your bow or quiver in front of the target. This action is especially important on a field course or bowhunting practice range where brush might hide you from the view of archers arriving to shoot that target.

FIGURE 2.4

**KEYS TO SUCCESS**

# RETRIEVING ARROWS SAFELY

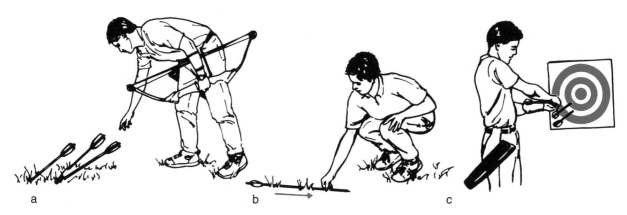

a                     b                     c

### Approaching the Target

1. Wait for signal to cross line ___
2. Walk to target ___
3. Watch for arrows in grass ___

### Retrieving Arrows

1. Pull forward any arrows embedded in the grass ___
2. Leave equipment in front of target if you walk behind target ___

### Removing Arrows From the Target

1. Make sure no one is behind you when removing arrows from the target ___
2. Twist arrows to remove them from target ___
3. Carry arrows in quiver ___

## SAFETY SUCCESS STOPPERS

Archery can be a very safe sport.  Act promptly to correct any situation that jeopardizes your safety or that of the archers and spectators around you.

| Error | Correction |
|---|---|
| 1.  Your bow dry fires (arrow falls to your feet on release). | 1.  Inspect the arrow nock for cracks. Replace cracked nocks. |
| 2.  Arrow flies erratically. | 2.  Avoid wearing baggy clothes that the bowstring may contact. Remove jewelry or pocket items on which the bowstring may catch. |
| 3.  The archer next to you steps in front of the shooting line. | 3.  Let your shot down (ease string forward). Remind archer to wait for the signal or all other archers to finish. |
| 4.  You must pick up a scorecard left below the target between ends. | 4.  Be careful not to poke your eye on the arrows in the target. In the future, place the scorecard to the side of the target. |
| 5.  You are shooting alone and carry your equipment behind the target to retrieve an arrow. | 5.  Leave your bow in front of the target as a signal to other archers. |

## SAFETY

# DRILLS

### 1. Safety Test

You should demonstrate your knowledge of the safety rules of archery before shooting your first arrows. For your sake and the sake of others learning archery with you, you must know and obey safety rules. Use the following questions to check your safety knowledge. Jot down your answers in the space provided.

**Before Shooting**

1. What should you do if you find a crack in your bow limb?

2. What should you do if you find a crack in a wood arrow?

3. What should you do if you find a crack in the plastic nock on your arrow?

4. How should you dress for shooting?

5. For what should your bowstring be checked?

## While Shooting

6. When is it safe to nock an arrow when shooting with a group?

7. When is it safe to nock an arrow when shooting on your own?

8. What does one whistle blast mean?

9. What do two whistle blasts mean?

10. What do three whistle blasts mean?

11. When is it permissible to step across the shooting line?

12. What should you do if your arrow falls off the arrow rest as you are drawing (pulling the bowstring back) or aiming?

13. When is it permissible to hold an arrow on the bow with your index finger?

## After Shooting

14. What should you do when you finish shooting your arrows?

15. How should the target be approached?

16. When should you retrieve arrows that fall short of the target?

17. When should you retrieve arrows that land behind the target?

18. For what should you check before pulling your arrows from the target?

*Success Goal* = 18 correct answers ___

## ✔ Success Check

1. Do not shoot; seek advice at a pro shop ___
2. Break it into two pieces and discard ___
3. Remove cracked nock and replace it (see appendix A) ___
4. Wear close-fitting clothing and remove jewelry and pocket items; tie hair back ___
5. Fraying or a broken strand, frayed serving ___
6. After signal (one whistle blast) ___
7. After checking for a clear target area ___
8. It is permissible to nock an arrow and begin shooting ___
9. It is permissible to cross line to retrieve arrows ___
10. Stop shooting immediately, emergency situation ___
11. After two whistle blasts, or when all archers have stepped back from line ___
12. Ease the string forward and start the shot over ___
13. Never! ___
14. Step back from the line and place your bow in the designated area ___
15. At a walk, watching for arrows that landed in the grass ___
16. On the way to the target ___
17. After positioning a fellow archer or your bow or quiver in front of the target ___
18. Archers or spectators standing in the way ___

## 2. Equipment Inspection

You should develop an inspection routine that you conduct before every shooting session. Follow these steps:

1. Inspect bow limbs for cracks.
2. Inspect arrow rest for breakage/slippage.
3. Make sure bowstrings and compound bow cables are seated properly.
4. Inspect bowstring and its serving for fraying or breakage.
5. Check arrows for cracks in shafts or nocks, and make sure the arrows' points are in place.

**Success Goal** = Create an inspection routine to examine your equipment for safety ___

## ✔ Success Check

• Cracked equipment set aside ___
• Bowstring and cable properly seated ___
• Bowstring and its serving without frays ___

## SAFETY SUCCESS SUMMARY

Every archer wants shooting to be an enjoyable experience for children and adults alike. Archers should never place someone in harm's way. Despite the inherent danger of the bow and arrow, shooting can be safe when all archers do two basic things: methodically and regularly inspect their equipment, and anticipate unsafe shooting conditions in order to correct them before shooting. Ask your teacher, your coach, or a friend to evaluate your safety knowledge according to the Keys to Success checklists in figures 2.1, 2.3, and 2.4.

# STEP 3

# SHOOTING FORM: USING "T" AS YOUR MODEL

S ome sports and sports skills are fun to play and watch because you never know what's going to happen next. Wrestlers have an ongoing interchange of attack and counterattack; soccer players switch from offense to defense and back to offense within seconds; volleyball players dig the ball one minute and spike it the next.

Other sports and sports skills are performed well only if they are executed the same way, correctly, every time. Like a great free throw shooter whose every attempt looks like a replay of the one preceding it, a successful archer is a consistent archer. An archer's goal is to establish perfect form, called T-form, and then reproduce it on every subsequent shot.

Note that we're referring to consistency in technique, not outcome, at least at first. So don't be distracted by the flight of the arrow. Instead, learn the T-form shooting technique taught in this step, and practice the drills to develop a shot pattern you will use every time you take aim. If you think that sounds boring, just think how bored you'll be with bull's-eye after bull's-eye!

## Why Is T-Form Important?

The body's muscle structure can maintain good T-form alignment of the arms and trunk with less effort than other positions. Muscle groups on opposite sides of the limbs and trunk pull evenly in T-form. Archers who assume bent positions at full draw are pulling more with one muscle than another. They may find it difficult to assume that exact position on subsequent shots, especially when they are fatigued or nervous. Remember that in shooting archery, you maintain your position for several seconds to aim while holding the bow up and the bowstring back against many pounds of resistance. The nervousness you may feel from wanting to shoot well in a contest, or the excitement you may feel as a deer is approaching, also could cause a breakdown in your form. You need a shooting style that is easy to reproduce, even under pressure.

It is also easier for you to visualize placing your body into the T-shape than a bent shape (see figure 3.1). You have an exact visual image of the T's straight

**Figure 3.1** Visualizing T-form.

44

lines and right angles. If your body or limbs are in a bent position, you can more easily adjust to a straight position than a degree of bend. So you can monitor your own form more easily when your goal is T-form.

You may see other archers experiencing some degree of success in shooting without T-form. This success might be short-lived. In the long run, archers with T-form are more comfortable and relaxed and shoot more accurately than archers without this alignment. Practicing T-form and making it a habit is well worth the effort in your early experience with archery.

## How to Mimic a T-Form Shot

The best way to learn the basic T-form shot is to first mimic it without actually shooting an arrow. Mimicking gives you the chance to make the motions of shooting habitual and to get used to the equipment gradually. Mimicking contributes to safe shooting, too. You can make sure you are handling the bow and arrow safely and not overdrawing the arrow.

Mimic T-form first without an arrow. Take a stance with your bow arm side toward the target, feet shoulder-width apart, and weight even. Check your stance by imagining a straight line going through the toes of each foot. If this line would continue toward your target, you are in good position (see figure 3.2a). If it would not, adjust your position. Stand straight and keep your shoulders square over your feet. Avoid twisting your trunk.

Hold the bow at the handle straight up and down in front of you. Form a hook with the middle three fingers of your string hand. Hook the bowstring in the end joint of the fingers with one finger above the nocking point and two below it (see figure 3.2b).

Raise and extend your bow arm at shoulder level toward the target. Look over your front shoulder. Draw the string by pulling your elbow back in one fluid motion. The shoulder blade of the drawing arm should move toward your spine. Remember, you will need to exert enough muscle force to overcome the draw weight of the bow. Bring the string hand back to your anchor position and rotate your bow elbow down and out (see figure 3.2c). The anchor position is under your chin, with the top finger and chin touching and the string touching the tip of your nose and your chin. Hold this position for a few seconds, noticing how it feels, and then ease the string forward to the bow's relaxed position. Never release a bowstring unless there is an arrow in the bow because "dry firing" might damage the bow. Relax before repeating the process.

Now mimic T-form with an arrow. Take your stance as before. Nock an arrow just below the nock indicator on the string. The index (odd-color) feather or vane should be toward you. Place the shaft on the arrow rest. Form your string hand hook and place one finger above the arrow and two below it. Draw to your anchor position as before. Remember not to go past your anchor position because you might pull the arrow off the arrow rest. Hold this position for a few seconds, and then ease the bowstring forward. Rest, and then repeat this mimic.

You might be tempted to skip mimicking, but remember that learning T-form before you start worrying about where the arrow will go will reap benefits later. When an archer shoots with a draw position based on straight lines and right angles, accuracy is sure to follow. Once you can mimic T-form, apply that same form to shooting with an arrow. Some world-class archers mimic their shots as a warm-up before their shooting sessions, so don't be afraid to make mimicking a regular part of your archery practice.

FIGURE 3.2    KEYS TO SUCCESS

# MIMICKED SHOT

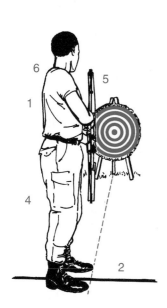

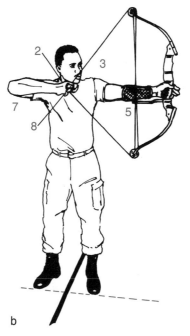

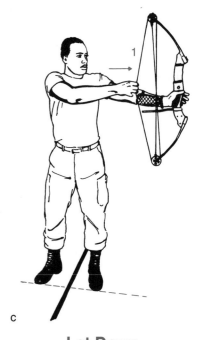

a

b

c

### Stance

1. Side toward target ___
2. Align feet ___
3. Weight even ___
4. Stand straight ___
5. Bow in front ___
6. Shoulders square ___
7. Mouth closed, teeth together ___

### Draw and Aim

1. Set bow in V of thumb and index finger ___
2. Set string hand hook ___
3. Look over front shoulder ___
4. Raise bow toward target___
5. Rotate bow elbow down ___
6. Relax string hand and wrist ___
7. Draw string elbow back at shoulder level ___
8. Chin on hand, string on chin and nose ___
9. Concentrate on target ___

### Let Down

1. Ease string forward ___

## How to Execute the T-Form Shot

Once you are comfortable mimicking T-form with an arrow, you need only add the release to shoot an arrow. Stand close (10 to 15 yards) to a target butt.

You can place a large target face or just a paper plate on the target butt for a focus point. At first, don't worry about where your arrows land.

Remember your safety rules. When you are sure the area behind and to the side of the target butt is clear, take your stance as in mimicking (see figure 3.3a). Set your bow and string hands just as before.

Draw and anchor (see figure 3.3b). Now tighten your back muscles and simply relax your fingers to release the string. Keep your bow arm up and head still (see figure 3.3c). The bow will do the rest!

After you have practiced the basic shot enough that you are comfortable drawing and releasing, add a predraw aim to your routine. A predraw aim places the bow arm at a height where the arrow tip is aligned

with a spot about 18 inches below the target. After anchoring, align the bowstring, which appears fuzzy when your aiming eye is focusing on the target, and the arrow shaft. Check the bow limbs through your peripheral vision to ensure that the bow is level. These two additions give you consistency in aiming your arrows vertically and horizontally.

**FIGURE 3.3**   KEYS TO SUCCESS

# T-FORM SHOT

a

b

c

## Stance

1. Side toward target ___
2. Align feet, weight even ___
3. Stand straight and square to target ___
4. Nock arrow against nock locator ___
5. Index feather toward you ___

## Draw and Aim

1. Set bow hand, then draw hand ___
2. One finger above, two fingers below arrow ___
3. Raise bow toward target ___
4. Rotate bow elbow down ___
5. Relax hands, draw hand flat ___
6. Move draw elbow back ___
7. Chin on hand, string on chin and nose ___
8. Align string and arrow shaft, level bow ___
9. Concentrate on target ___

## Release and Follow-Through

1. Tighten back muscles ___
2. Maintain relaxed bow and draw hands ___
3. Count to three ___
4. Relax draw hand to release string ___
5. Draw elbow pulls back on release ___
6. Keep bow arm up, toward target ___
7. Maintain head position ___
8. Draw hand finishes over rear shoulder ___

## SHOOTING FORM SUCCESS STOPPERS

Identifying your deviations from T-form might be difficult to do yourself. The drills that follow may help you to see some of your own errors. You can identify other errors from the actions of the arrow and bowstring.

| Error | Correction |
| --- | --- |
| 1. The hips slide forward and/or the front shoulder scrunches up. | 1. Stand straight and use the back muscles to draw by moving the draw elbow back. If you cannot make this correction, switch to a bow that is lighter in draw weight. |
| 2. Arrow falls off rest during draw. | 2. Keep the wrist and first knuckles of the draw hand straight throughout the draw. Use the hand only as a hook, moving the arm with the back muscles. Keep the bow vertical. |
| 3. At full draw, the draw elbow is facing to the side rather than back, away from the target. The elbow points down. | 3. Check that your feet are aligned with the imaginary line that travels straight to the target. Keep your shoulders square over your feet. Start the draw by moving the elbow back at shoulder level, not by flexing the forearm. |
| 4. Bowstring strikes bow arm above arm guard. | 4. Make sure the bow hand is directly behind the bow handle. Rotate the elbow down and out. If rotating the elbow still does not clear the arm, wear a long arm guard that covers both the forearm and upper arm. |
| 5. The arrow lifts up off the arrow rest. | 5. Pull evenly with your three fingers. |
| 6. Draw stops before reaching anchor point, and/or head is brought forward to meet string. | 6. Keep your head up and use the back muscles to draw in a fluid motion. Archers who draw too slowly tend to use more of their arm muscles than their back muscles. If you continue to have this problem, have a trained person check the fit of your bow, especially the draw weight of a recurve bow and the draw length of a compound bow. |

## SHOOTING FORM

# DRILLS

### 1. Bow Arm Drill

It is helpful to practice rotating your elbow down and out while there is pressure against your hand. Approach a doorjamb and extend your bow arm. (If you are outdoors with nothing to lean against, you can have a partner provide resistance.) Place the heel of your hand against the doorjamb (thumb toward ceiling) and lean against the doorjamb slightly. Rotate your elbow down and around without moving your hand, so that the wider part of your arm is vertical. Be sure to keep your bow shoulder down, not hunched. You can check your position by now bending your arm at the elbow. If your hand is at chest level, your elbow position has been correct. If your hand is at face level, your elbow position has been incorrect.

a

b

**◖ Success Goal** = 10 repetitions of rotating elbow, and then checking elbow position ___

**✔ Success Check**
• Level the shoulders ___
• Keep hand vertical ___
• Rotate elbow down and out ___

**To Increase Difficulty**
• Hold your bow and extend it toward a target.
• Hook the bowstring with your string hand and rotate the elbow down.

**To Decrease Difficulty**
• Hold your bow arm out to the side at shoulder level, palm down. Keeping your arm in place, rotate your hand to a vertical position. Your bow arm should be in proper position. Relax, and then try to achieve this position with the preceding drill.

## 2. Release Mimic

Without equipment, form your string hand hook. Hook it onto the forefinger of your bow hand and anchor under your chin. Tighten your back muscles, leaving your draw hand relaxed. Relax your fingers to "release." Your draw hand should be carried back toward your rear shoulder by your back tension. You can do this drill anywhere, anytime.

**◖ Success Goal** = 10 relaxed releases with string hand carried back toward rear shoulder ___

**✔ Success Check**
• String hand wrist and first knuckles straight ___
• Tighten back muscles ___
• Relax string fingers ___

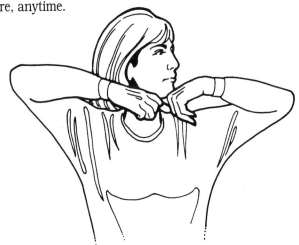

### 3. Mirror Drill

Standing diagonally in front of a mirror with a bow, practice setting your bow hand and a relaxed hook with your draw hand fingers. Raise the bow, and draw by moving your elbow straight back at shoulder level. Keep your draw wrist straight and relaxed. Be sure to anchor with the bowstring touching the middle of your nose and chin. Check your position for T-form by looking in the mirror; move just your eyes, not your head. Slowly ease the string back. Also try this drill with your eyes closed so you can focus on the feel of T-form.

**Success Goal** = 20 total draws ___
10 with eyes open ___
10 with eyes closed ___

✔ **Success Check**
• Level shoulders, head erect ___
• Move draw elbow back at shoulder level ___
• String hand touches chin, string touches nose and chin ___

**To Increase Difficulty**
• Repeat this drill with an arrow, but only if you can be positioned in front of a target backstop.

**To Decrease Difficulty**
• Perform this drill without a bow or with a bow much lighter in poundage than your shooting bow.

### 4. Partner Check

You will need a partner somewhat familiar with T-form for this drill. Place a paper plate in the middle of the target butt. Shoot an arrow from 10 yards with a partner watching from behind you, slightly to the side. Now shoot five arrows (called an *end*) using the same form from shot to shot. Your partner should try to catch you varying your form. You will probably find it more difficult to maintain form on your later arrows, as you tire. Don't worry about striking the plate; it is only a visual focus point. Retrieve your arrows and repeat the drill.

**Success Goal** = Duplicate the form used on your first arrow on 3 of the following 5 shots ___

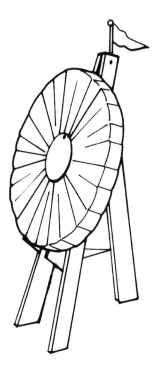

✔ *Success Check*
- Keep the bow arm and draw arm at shoulder level ___
- Anchor, string touches nose and chin ___
- Relax the draw hand to release, maintaining T-form ___

**To Increase Difficulty**
- Strive for identical form on all six arrows per end.

**To Decrease Difficulty**
- Mimic your shot with an arrow, but do not release.

## 5. Scoring Drill

Place a piece of white paper measuring approximately two feet by two feet on the target butt. Shoot an end of five arrows from a distance of 10 yards and note how many land on the paper to establish a standard. Now shoot four more ends.

*Success Goal* = 4 ends equaling or bettering the number of arrows hitting paper in the standard (first) end ___

✔ *Success Check*
- Relax the draw hand to release ___
- Maintain T-form ___

**To Increase Difficulty**
- Draw a tic-tac-toe pattern on the paper with a broad-tip marking pen. Write point values in the squares. Shoot five arrows at a time. Record the number of points earned by arrows landing in squares. Arrows touching a line can take the higher point value. Shoot five ends of five arrows each.

**To Decrease Difficulty**
- Use a larger piece of paper.

## 6. Target Drill

Place a traditional, multicolor archery target that is 80 centimeters in diameter on the target butt. Shoot five arrows at a time from 10 yards. Arrows score 10 for landing in the inner yellow bull's-eye, 9 for landing in the surrounding yellow circle, 8 for the next circle, and so on. Arrows touching a line can take the higher value. Shoot five ends of five arrows.

*Success Goal* = 4 ends with higher point values than your first end ___

✔ *Success Check*
- Align feet, stand straight, extend bow to target ___
- Move elbow back at shoulder level ___
- Settle, and then relax string fingers ___

*To Increase Difficulty*
- Shoot from 15 yards.

*To Decrease Difficulty*
- Use a 120 centimeter target.

### 7. Balloon Pop

Blow up six balloons and mount them on a target butt. Shooting five arrows per end from a distance of 10 yards, try to pop as many balloons as possible. When you pop them all, place another six balloons on the target butt and repeat the drill.

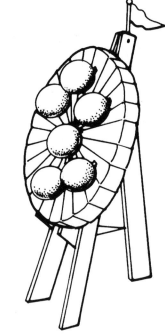

 *Success Goal* = Pop all 6 balloons within 3 ends ___

✔ *Success Check*
- T-form ___
- Relax bow and string hands ___
- Settle, and then relax ___

*To Increase Difficulty*
- Shoot from 12 yards.
- Use fewer balloons or spread the balloons out.

*To Decrease Difficulty*
- Use more balloons.
- Place balloons closer together.

## SHOOTING FORM SUCCESS SUMMARY

You have been practicing the archery shot with T-form, which stresses straight lines and right angles. The sooner you make T-form a habit, the sooner you will achieve success in hitting your target! The practice drills in this step provide a variety of ways to make T-form a habit, so by now you should be comfortable getting a shot off.

You probably noticed that the more consistent your T-form became, the more your arrows grouped rather than scattered on the target. An experienced archer can group arrows even if blindfolded, just by relying on the feel of habitually practiced T-form. Ask your teacher, coach, or a friend to evaluate your form according to the Keys to Success checklists in figures 3.2 and 3.3.

# STEP 4

## AIMING: ZEROING IN ON YOUR MARK WITH A BOWSIGHT

At the World Target Championships, archer Park, Kyung-Mo found himself shooting against a former world champion in the semifinal match. From 70 meters, he shot his first two arrows into the 10 ring, which is the inner part of the gold bull's-eye. The next arrow was a 9, landing in the outer part of the bull's-eye, but the remaining nine arrows all landed in the 10 ring. Park, Kyung-Mo's score of 119 points out of 120 possible points established a new world record, and he went on to take first place.

Many years of practice helped Park, Kyung-Mo establish a world record, but certain equipment accessories helped him as well. The most important of these accessories was a bowsight. A bowsight helps you direct your bow in a consistent direction from shot to shot. Once the bowsight is set, it also tells archers where to direct the bow to shoot at targets or at game that are varying distances away. Although some archers enjoy the challenge of shooting without a bowsight, most target archers and bowhunters use one. In this step, you will learn how to aim with a bowsight.

## How Does a Bowsight Improve Accuracy?

With a bowsight, you can direct your arrows to the same spot on the target from shot to shot. You can reproduce the alignment used on any one shot because you align an aiming aperture on the bowsight with the bull's-eye. If your arrows hit outside the bull's-eye, you can use the bowsight as a calibrated means of adjustment for subsequent shots. You can adjust the bowsight both horizontally and vertically; you must previously establish through trial and er-

ror just how great an adjustment is needed. When you change shooting distance, move the bowsight vertically—down for a greater distance, up for a shorter distance. This adjustment changes the height of your bow arm and consequently the trajectory of the arrow. The horizontal adjustment allows you to accommodate slight changes in shooting form that direct the arrow to the right or left and to adjust for shooting conditions, including wind.

## How to Use a Bowsight

The principles of using a bowsight are the same whether you have a simple, homemade sight, a hunting sight, or a sophisticated tournament sight. You aim the sight aperture at the bull's-eye on every shot. Your shooting form is basically the same as you have been practicing, but you need to add several steps that are related to aligning the bowsight.

After taking your stance (see figure 4.1a), drawing, and anchoring, align the sight aperture and bull's-eye using the eye on the draw hand side of your body. Remember that if your other eye is dominant, you may need to close it so that you use only the string side eye for aiming. Level the bow, and then adjust your head position so that you see the string running down the middle of the bow. The string should be just to the right, for a right-handed archer, of the aperture (see figure 4.1b). Your eye should bring the bull's-eye into focus, permitting the aperture and bowstring to blur slightly. Wait until the sight aperture is steady in the middle of the bull's-eye. This usually takes several seconds. When the aperture is steady and aligned, tighten your back muscles and relax your string hand to release the string (see figure 4.1c). You will be able to hold the sight more steady as you practice and develop greater muscle strength. However, archers can rarely stop the aperture "dead" in the bull's-eye; attempting to do so usually results in too much tension in the bow and string hands. If you are using a peep sight, which is discussed in step 1, look through the peep sight and make sure the bull's-eye is centered in the opening rather than aligning the string as described.

| FIGURE 4.1 | KEYS TO SUCCESS |
|---|---|

# SHOOTING WITH A BOWSIGHT

a

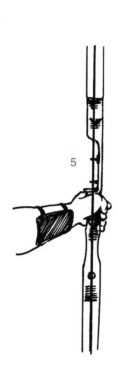

b

c

### Stance

1. Assume stance ___
2. Nock arrow ___
3. Set bow and string hands ___

### Draw and Aim

1. Draw and anchor ___
2. Close eye opposite string side, if necessary ___
3. Align string side eye with sight and bull's-eye ___
4. Level bow ___
5. Adjust head to see string bisecting bow and aligning just to right of aperture, or center target in peep sight ___
6. Focus on bull's-eye ___
7. Steady sight aperture in center of bull's-eye ___

### Release and Follow-Through

1. Tighten back muscles ___
2. Relax string hand to release ___
3. Keep bow arm up ___
4. Keep head steady and focus on bull's-eye ___

# How to Adjust the Aiming Aperture

You establish the proper horizontal and vertical position of the aiming aperture by trial and error. After you shoot several arrows, observe their location on the target face. Move the aperture in the direction of error (see figure 4.2). For example, if the arrows group low, move the sight aperture down; sighting through a lower aperture results in your holding your bow arm and, consequently, your bow higher. If the arrows group high, move the sight aperture up. If the arrows group left, move the aperture left. Be sure to make left/right adjustments with the bowsight oriented to the target.

When a sight setting is off, some archers are tempted to aim outside the bull's-eye to compensate rather than adjusting the position of the sight. Aiming off-center is less desirable than moving the sight, unless sight movements are restricted by the rules for a particular class or style of competitive shooting. Consistently finding any position on a target other than the center of the bull's-eye is almost impossible. Don't hesitate to move your sight. That is why it is adjustable! However, if you feel that you varied from T-form on a particular shot, don't make a sight adjustment based on where that arrow landed. Wait to analyze the position of an arrow shot with good T-form.

If you move to a longer distance, you need to move your bowsight down so that your bow arm is directed to give your shot a higher trajectory. Naturally, if you move closer, you need to raise your sight. How far you move your sight for a given change in distance is established first by trial and error. Thereafter, you can keep a written record of the setting for a particular distance.

Changing distances does not necessitate a horizontal adjustment of your sight. Small errors in the position of your sight, though, have a more apparent effect at longer distances. For example, if your arrows fall on the right side of, but still in, the bull's-eye when shooting from 20 yards, they likely would fall to the right of, but outside, the bull's-eye at 50 yards. Therefore, some horizontal adjustment of your bowsight might be necessary as you change distances.

Target archers typically use a bowsight with a single aperture that slides up and down the sight. A scale on the sight enables archers to establish a chart of sight positions corresponding to various distances. Bowhunters do not have the time to reposition their sights for a given distance, even if their game is nice enough to stand still! A hunting sight usually has four- or five-pin apertures that can be positioned for those distances the archer is likely to need. The hunter estimates the distance to game and selects the appropriate pin to use in aiming.

The aperture on a target or hunting sight can vary in its configuration. You may want to try several and choose one based on personal preference. Some archers prefer an open ring in which to center the bull's-eye; others prefer crosshairs or a point to center on their targets. You may want to shoot in a particular tournament classification that has restrictive rules on bowsights and sight apertures. At one extreme, some archers use apertures with a magnifying lens, a lighted center point, and a level. Others use a plain, open ring.

FIGURE
4.2 **KEYS TO SUCCESS**

# ADJUSTING THE AIMING APERTURE

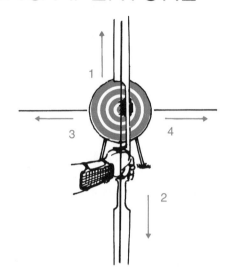

1. Move bowsight up if arrows group above bull's-eye ___
2. Move bowsight down if arrows group below bull's-eye ___
3. Move bowsight left if arrows group left of bull's-eye ___
4. Move bowsight right if arrows group right of bull's-eye ___

## AIMING SUCCESS STOPPERS

It is tempting to think that using a bowsight will result in the perfect shot every time. But remember that consistency, even consistency in aiming, is fundamental to accurate shooting. You can identify sight and aiming errors both by where your arrows land on the target and by your actions in executing the shot.

| Error | Correction |
|---|---|
| 1. Some of your arrows land to the right or left of the bull's-eye. | 1. Align the bowstring with the middle of the bow limbs and just to the right of the sight aperture on every shot. |
| 2. Your arrows sometimes land to the right of the bull's-eye. | 2. Maintain your visual focus on the bull's-eye until the arrow hits the target. Peeking to watch the arrow often moves the bow to the right. |
| 3. You aim the sight aperture off-center to compensate for where the arrows land on the target. | 3. Aim at the center of the bull's-eye every shot and move your sight to compensate for where the arrows land. |
| 4. Your arrows land farther from the bull's-eye after a sight adjustment than before. | 4. Be sure you moved your sight in the direction of the arrows' error with the bow oriented to the target as when you shoot. |
| 5. Your arrows horizontally spread across the target. | 5. If you shoot with both eyes open, recheck for your dominant eye (see step 1). Try closing your bow side eye. |
| 6. Your arrows group away from the bull's-eye. | 6. Move your sight in the direction of the grouping of arrows with your bowsight oriented toward the target. |

AIMING

# DRILLS

### *1. Aiming Mimic*

Some archers tend to release the bowstring as soon as the sight is on the bull's-eye, instead of steadying the aperture and aiming. Without using an arrow, practice drawing, aligning your string and sight, steadying your aperture, and aiming from a distance of 20 yards. Aim for a count of at least three, and then ease the string back.

**Success Goal** = 10 repetitions with steady aiming ___

✓ **Success Check**
- Align string to right of aperture or center peep sight ___
- Focus on bull's-eye ___
- Steady aperture in center of bull's-eye ___

**To Increase Difficulty**
- Put up a three-spot target face (a target with three sets of the 6, 7, 8, 9, and 10 rings) or a large sheet of paper with three bull's-eyes drawn on it. From 10 to 20 yards, draw to align the string and center the sight. After you have steadied your aperture on the first bull's-eye, move to the second bull's-eye, align, steady, aim, move to the third bull's eye, align, steady, aim, and then let down the bow and relax. Repeat this sequence at least 10 times. You can let down the bow after the second bull's-eye if you tire.

## 2. Sight Adjustment Practice

In this drill, you practice designating the direction of sight adjustment. The location of a group of arrows is given in terms of a clockface. Fill in the direction(s) of sight adjustment needed to bring subsequent shots to the center of the target.

Example: For a group at 4 o'clock, adjust right and down.

1. For a group at 6 o'clock, adjust _____

2. For a group at 8 o'clock, adjust _____

3. For a group at 1 o'clock, adjust _____

4. For a group at 3 o'clock, adjust _____

5. For a group at 11 o'clock, adjust _____

**Success Goal** = Make the correct sight adjustment in every situation ____

**Success Check**
- Orient bowsight toward target, as when shooting ____
- Adjust in the direction of the arrow group ____
- Make the correct adjustments ____
  1. down
  2. left and down
  3. up and right
  4. right
  5. up and left

## 3. Sighting In

Shoot from a short distance of 15 yards, using an 80 centimeter target face. Shoot three arrows using an initial sight setting with the aperture high on the sight bar. Note where the three arrows land and adjust your sight. Continue shooting and adjusting until your arrows group around the bull's-eye. Record the location of this sight setting in the following Success Goal section. Now move to 20 yards and repeat this process. When you have established a sight setting, record it. Continue this process, moving back in 5-yard increments to a distance of 40 yards. You can anticipate the needed sight adjustment by moving your sight down a small amount each time you increase your distance from the target.

**Success Goal** = Establish a sight setting for every distance from 15 to 40 yards in 5-yard increments ____

15 yard sight setting: _____

20 yard sight setting: _____

25 yard sight setting: _____

30 yard sight setting: _____

35 yard sight setting: _____

40 yard sight setting: _____

**Success Check**
- Move your sight down as you move back ____
- Make sight corrections after shots with good form, not bad ____

### 4. Quick Sight Move

Place an 80 centimeter target on the target butt. Start at 40 yards and shoot a six-arrow end. Record your score, and then move to 35 yards and shoot another end. Continue moving closer to the target in 5-yard increments until you have completed an end at 20 yards. Now move back to 40 yards and repeat the process.

**Success Goal** = Improve your score in the second round over the first round ___

|  | Round 1 | Round 2 |
|---|---|---|
| 40 yards | _____ | _____ |
| 35 yards | _____ | _____ |
| 30 yards | _____ | _____ |
| 25 yards | _____ | _____ |
| 20 yards | _____ | _____ |
| Total | _____ | _____ |

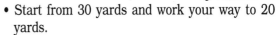

**To Increase Difficulty**
• Use a smaller target.
• Start from 50 yards.

### To Decrease Difficulty
• Start from 30 yards and work your way to 20 yards.
• Use a larger target.

**Success Check**
• Move your sight up as you move closer to the target ___
• Move your sight in the direction of the arrows' errors ___

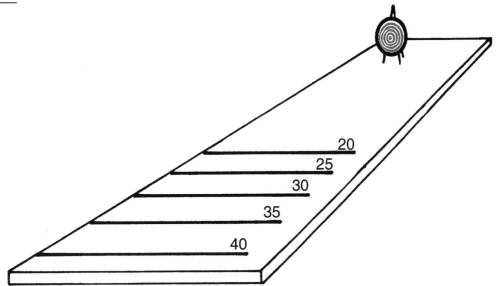

## 5. Subtraction

Choose a partner. Place an 80 centimeter target on the target butt. Each of you should place a piece of tape around one of your arrows. Shoot from 30 yards. On each of four ends, total your five unmarked arrows. Then, subtract the value of your marked arrow from your opponent's score.

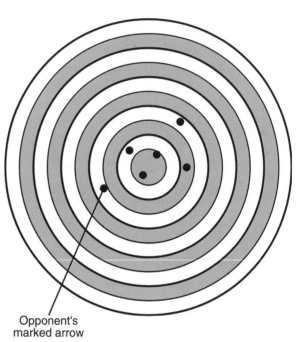

Opponent's marked arrow

**Success Goal** = Outscore your partner \_\_\_\_

End 1: \_\_\_\_pts−\_\_\_\_pts = _____   Partner: _____
End 2: \_\_\_\_pts−\_\_\_\_pts = _____   Partner: _____
End 3: \_\_\_\_pts−\_\_\_\_pts = _____   Partner: _____
End 4: \_\_\_\_pts−\_\_\_\_pts = _____   Partner: _____
Total:                 _____   Partner: _____

**Success Check**

• Align your bowstring on every shot \_\_\_\_
• Let the sight aperture settle in the bull's-eye \_\_\_\_
• Focus on the middle of the bull's-eye \_\_\_\_

**To Increase Difficulty**

• Shoot from 35 yards.

**To Decrease Difficulty**

• Shoot from 25 yards.
• Use a larger target.

## AIMING SUCCESS SUMMARY

After learning to use a bowsight in this step, your shooting is more accurate than before, especially at longer distances. Of course, simply having a bowsight does not mean you will always hit the bull's-eye. Ask a teacher or friend to evaluate your technique according to the Keys to Success checklist in figure 4.1. If you are aiming and adjusting your bowsight correctly, and your arrows still land off-center, continue to refine your basic T-form. Make sight adjustments only after well-executed shots. Once your technique matches the checklist in figure 4.1, you can still improve through better concentration during the aiming phase of your shot. Use the Keys to Success checklist in figure 4.2 to sight in as you change shooting distances.

# STEP

## 5 SHOT REFINEMENT: BULL'S-EYE BOUND

F ew sports can take as many forms as archery: target shooting, field shooting, distance shooting, bowhunting, and bowfishing. You are probably anxious to try one or more of these forms. As you choose a specific type of archery, you will need to refine your T-form to be the most compatible with the goal of that style of archery. For example, getting a shot off quickly is more important in bowhunting than in target archery. Establishing an anchor position quickly becomes crucial to success in bowhunting.

Refining your shooting form to a personal style also accommodates your body shape and structure. For example, you might choose a certain bow hand position because it is the most comfortable and consistent for your arm and wrist or a certain stance because you are more heavy-chested than the average shooter. Refining the more detailed aspects of your shooting style will take your performance to a higher level. Your practice drills must emphasize exact positions and replication of each aspect of your refined form. In this step, you will refine three parts of your shooting style: your stance, your bow hand position, and your anchor position.

## Why Is It Important to Vary Your Stance?

As part of basic T-form, you took a stance with your feet about shoulder-width apart and your toes along an imaginary line that goes straight to the target. This stance is known as the square stance. The square stance is a good stance for beginners because it is natural, easy to establish, and easy to duplicate. However, every archer also has a unique natural stance, a stance that feels the most comfortable. Your body build often dictates that one stance is better than another for you. You must experiment to find the stance that enables you to naturally direct the bow straight to the target without drifting right or left.

## How to Vary Your Stance

The three basic archery stances are square, open, and closed. The square stance places the toes on a line straight to the target (see figure 5.1a). The open stance (see figure 5.1b) moves the rear foot up across this imaginary line (a position that opens the body to the target), and the closed stance moves the front foot up across this line (see figure 5.1c). You should determine whether to open or close your stance and by how much. Each stance has advantages and disadvantages (see table 5.1).

Stand 20 yards from a target with a square stance. Without actually shooting an arrow, draw and anchor, aim, then close your eyes and count to three. Open them and note whether the sight has drifted to the left or right. If it drifted to the right (and you are shooting right-handed), open your stance a little; if it drifted to the left, close your stance a little. Repeat this process, correcting your foot position a little each time, until your bow remains steady. Once you find this natural stance, you may want to use footmarkers to promote consistency until the stance becomes second nature.

## Why Is It Important to Choose a Bow Hand Position?

You can use one of several bow hand positions: the low wrist, the high wrist, or the straight wrist. With each bow hand position, archers strive to maintain a relaxed bow hand so that they resist the push of the bow on their bow arm as the bowstring is drawn rather than grip their bow. Archers choose the hand

**FIGURE 5.1**  **KEYS TO SUCCESS**

# STANCE

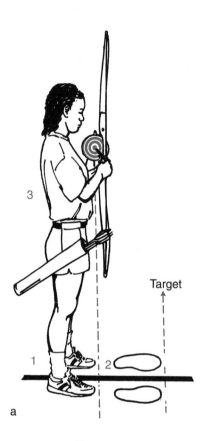

a

### Square

1. Feet shoulder-width apart ___
2. Toes aligned ___
3. Body erect ___
4. Weight even ___

b

### Open

1. Front foot turned outward 45 degrees ___
2. Rear foot forward six inches ___
3. Body erect ___
4. Square shoulders ___
5. Weight even ___
6. Line to target intersects middle of rear foot, toes of front foot ___

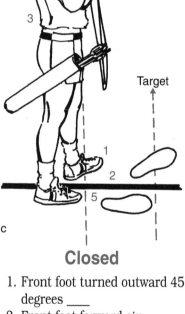

c

### Closed

1. Front foot turned outward 45 degrees ___
2. Front foot forward six inches ___
3. Body erect ___
4. Weight even ___
5. Line to target intersects toes of rear foot, middle of front foot ___

position that best allows them to maintain a relaxed hold, given their strength and bone and muscle structure. If you have not yet used a bow or finger sling, do so now (see step 1). With a sling, you are not as tempted to grip the bow as without one.

Any movement of the bow as the arrow is clearing the arrow rest can cause a deviation in where the arrow lands. Consider that pushing the tail end of an arrow just one degree off center can make it land far from the bull's-eye. You want to avoid any movement of the bow at the time of release. If your bow hand is tense or grips the bow in a tight hold, you are more likely to move upon release than if your bow hand is relaxed.

| Table 5.1 | Advantages and Disadvantages of Various Stances | |
|---|---|---|
| **Type of stance** | **Advantages** | **Disadvantages** |
| **Square** | Natural position<br>Easy to duplicate | Small base of support in front-to-back (sagittal) plane<br>Body can sway, especially in windy conditions<br>Minimizes string clearance, especially for heavy-chested shooters |
| **Open** | Provides stable base of support<br>Minimizes tendency to lean away from target<br>Provides more string clearance than other stances | Promotes tendency to twist upper body to face target<br>Promotes tendency to use arm more than back muscles to draw |
| **Closed** | Provides stable base of support<br>Promotes good alignment of arm and shoulder in direct line to target | Minimizes string clearance; string may strike body or clothing<br>Promotes tendency to lean away from target or overdraw |

Many archers also have a tendency to grab the bow as they release the string, even if their bow hand is relaxed during draw and aiming. This turning of the bow, or torque, can still affect the tail end of the arrow as it clears the arrow rest. Also, beginning archers sometimes anticipate the release so that the bow is moving throughout the release of the bowstring. Only dedicated practice relaxing the bow hand throughout the shot and follow-through can overcome these errors.

Another reason for maintaining a relaxed bow hand is that your two hands tend to mirror one another in tension level. If your bow hand is tight, your string hand tends to be tight as well. If your bow hand is relaxed, your string hand tends to be relaxed, too, resulting in a cleaner release of the string.

## How to Choose the Bow Hand Position

The three bow hand positions put the wrist at a different height in relation to the bow hand. The low position places your arm below your bow hand (see figure 5.2a), and the high position places your arm above your hand (see figure 5.2b). The arm and hand form a line in the straight wrist position (see figure 5.2c). In the low and straight positions, the hand is placed so that the pressure is along the inner side of the thumb muscle.

Regardless of which wrist position minimizes torque and bow movement the best for you, the three positions have common features. First, an imaginary line running down the center of the bow arm should intersect the center of the bow. This alignment brings the line of pressure closest to the line of pressure exerted by the bowstring, making torque easier to control. Second, your hand and fingers must be completely relaxed so that the bow jumps forward upon release (and is caught by the bow sling) rather than turning to the right or left. As a result, the bowstring should travel a straighter line as it accelerates the arrow, and the arrow should clear the bow without interference.

Which position you use is largely a matter of preference, but you may find that your physical strength and structure lends itself to a particular bow hand position. Also, the shape of the bow's handle or grip can determine a particular bow hand position. Some bows are made with removable hand grips so that you can install the hand grip shape that allows you to use your preferred bow hand position. Experiment with the various bow hand positions to determine the best one for you, but note that each has advantages and disadvantages (see table 5.2).

FIGURE
5.2 **KEYS TO SUCCESS**

# WRIST POSITIONS

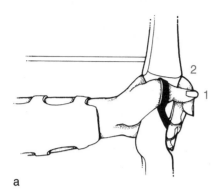

a

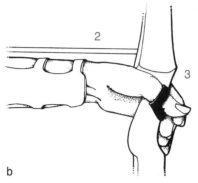

b

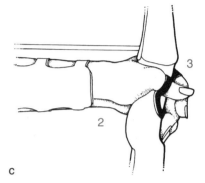

c

### Low Wrist

1. Hand on bow, pressure along inner side of thumb, knuckles at 45-degree angle ___
2. Bow rests on base of thumb ___
3. Center line of arm intersects center of bow ___
4. Relax wrist backward as bow is drawn ___
5. Relax hand and fingers ___

### High Wrist

1. Center line of arm intersects center of bow ___
2. Wrist higher than hand ___
3. Pressure of bow on small area of hand ___
4. Relax hand and fingers ___

### Straight Wrist

1. Center line of arm intersects center of bow ___
2. Wrist level with hand ___
3. Pressure of bow on web of hand ___
4. Relax hand and fingers ___

| Table 5.2 | Advantages and Disadvantages of Various Wrist Positions | |
|---|---|---|
| Type of wrist position | Advantages | Disadvantages |
| Low | Allows wrist to relax backward completely<br>Does not require great wrist strength | Promotes tendency to grab bow if wrist and fingers are not relaxed |
| High | Minimizes area of hand contacting bow handle<br>Minimizes bow torque<br>Minimizes tendency to grab bow on release | Difficult to maintain over long shooting session without great strength<br>Promotes tendency to move wrist at release with fatigue |
| Straight | Consistent from shot to shot<br>Makes deviations in position easy to feel | Difficult to maintain over long shooting session without great strength<br>Pressure against skin web between thumb and forefinger promotes tendency to wrap fingers around bow |

## Why Is It Important to Vary Your Anchor?

The under-chin anchor used thus far is a common one, but it may not be the one best suited for your body structure or the type and style of archery you prefer. In the under-chin anchor, the string always touches the tip of the nose and the chin. Some archers place the string in the center of the chin; others place it to the side of the chin. Placing the string in the center of the chin necessitates tipping the head, which is an uncomfortable position for some archers. Archers with large hands or short necks sometimes find it difficult to use the under-chin anchor. Time is also needed to anchor under the chin, and this factor is a disadvantage in bowhunting.

Some archers use another variation of the under-chin anchor where they put the thumb behind the neck. Although positioning the anchor this way takes time, this anchor variation minimizes the problem of the string creeping forward at release.

To offset the disadvantages of the under-chin anchor, many archers use a side anchor, which involves anchoring the hand and bowstring to the side of the chin. This anchor is comfortable, allows for a natural head position, and is quickly established. For these reasons, it is a favorite among hunters.

Using a release aid affects your anchor position as well. You might decide to shoot with a release aid because it is more accurate than a finger release. In addition, hunting bows are often designed to be short so that they can be easily carried and used in forested areas. This design results in a more acute bowstring angle at full draw, which tends to pinch the fingers. Shooting with a release aid helps you avoid this discomfort.

## How to Use the Various Anchor Positions

Anchor positions depend on touch points that you re-establish on every shot. Anchor positions vary in how many and which touch points are used, but most of them use the tip of the nose as a touch point. Unless you can be absolutely sure of replicating another anchor position on every shot, use an anchor that has the string touching the tip of the nose. If you use a peep sight, this touch point is less important. The peep sight is always aligned so that you see the bull's-eye and bowsight in the center of the peep sight's opening.

The anchor position you have been using is termed the under-chin anchor (see figure 5.3a). Many archers who use the under-chin anchor place their thumb or little finger on their neck. This position assures an anchor that is close to the neck, keeping the arrow and bow arm more in line to the target. If you decide to continue with this anchor, try adding one of these touch points.

You might prefer to anchor on the side of your face (see figure 5.3b). You can use the side anchor in a high or low position, depending on the accessories you use. If you are not using a peep sight or kisser button, anchor to the side by placing the tip of your index finger in the corner of your mouth. If you are using a kisser button, place the kisser button between your lips in the corner of your mouth. Your string hand is lower, with the index finger anchored under your jawbone. Place your nose on the string for an extra reference point, even if you use a kisser button. You can use the low side anchor without a kisser button by letting the string cross the corner of your mouth. Take care to reproduce this anchor as precisely as possible from shot to shot.

You may like shooting with a release aid, the mechanical device that holds the bowstring until the archer triggers the release (see figure 5.3c). The release aid anchor varies with the type of release aid used, but this anchor almost always establishes a touch point on the neck or jaw because the trigger mechanism that holds the string places the hand farther back. You might want to try a different anchor, but remember that accurate shooting requires an anchor that can be precisely replicated on every shot. You must hold caliper release aids vertically. You can hold rope release aids in virtually any orientation you prefer. Some archers even turn their palm away from their face so they may place their knuckles behind their jawbone.

With any anchor, your draw should be straight back in the plane intersecting the target, not out and then in. The anchor should be close to the neck and identically positioned on every shot. Your hand should be relaxed throughout the shot. When you use proper back tension, the follow-through of the release will always be back over the rear shoulder, no matter what

FIGURE
5.3 **KEYS TO SUCCESS**

# ANCHOR POSITIONS

a

b

c

### Under-Chin

1. Bring draw elbow back ___
2. Draw close to bow arm ___
3. Draw hand under chin ___
4. Touch string to nose and chin ___
5. Touch kisser button between lips ___
6. Align peep sight, if used ___
7. Relax back of hand ___
8. Keep wrist straight ___

### Side

1. Bring draw elbow back ___
2. Draw straight back to side of face ___
3. Draw hand to side of face ___
4. Touch string to nose ___
5. Touch kisser button or index finger to corner of mouth ___
6. Align peep sight, if used ___
7. Relax back of hand ___
8. Keep wrist straight ___

### Release Aid

1. Bring draw elbow back ___
2. Draw close to bow arm ___
3. Touch hand to face or neck ___
4. Touch string to nose ___
5. Touch kisser button to corner of mouth or align peep sight ___
6. Place finger on trigger ___
7. Increase back tension ___

type of anchor you use. Be aware of the advantages and disadvantages of each type of anchor (see table 5.3). Keep in mind that the rear position of the arrow anchors the trajectory of the shot. Varying the tra-jectory by varying the anchor from shot to shot sends each arrow to a different place on the target. Once you select your anchor position, keep and perfect it.

## Table 5.3 Advantages and Disadvantages of Various Anchor Positions

| Type of anchor | Advantages | Disadvantages |
|---|---|---|
| **Under-chin** | Two touch points aid consistency | Uncomfortable for archer with large hands or short neck |
| | Prevents overdrawing | Takes time to position |
| | Low position on face allows long distance shots with less sight movement, especially with lightweight bow | Tips head |
| **Side** | Position is quickly established | Permits overdrawing |
| | Allows sighting down arrow shaft when shooting barebow | Permits creeping |
| **Release aid** | Extremely accurate | Requires separate tuning setup of bow |
| | Comfortable | Release aids are additional expense |
| | Longer effective draw length | Trigger models might lead to flinching |

## SHOT REFINEMENT SUCCESS STOPPERS

In archery, you can easily overlook how much difference minute aspects of form make in performance. Archers who attend to the details of establishing a good base of support, using a bow hand position that eliminates bow arm movement at release, and anchoring in the same place on every shot will experience success. If you find yourself making the errors listed here, focus on the smallest detail to make the correction.

| Error | Correction |
|---|---|
| ***Stance*** | |
| 1. Foot position varies from shot to shot or end to end. | 1. Use footmarkers. Golf tees work outdoors; use chalk or tape indoors. |
| 2. You feel tension in your draw arm when using the open stance. | 2. Rotate upper body if necessary to square shoulders to the target. |
| 3. You lean away from the target when using the closed stance. | 3. Make sure your weight is evenly distributed on both feet. When using a closed stance, make sure your body is erect; consider opening stance slightly. |

| Error | Correction |
|---|---|
| **Bow Hand Position** | |
| 1. Knuckles are white during hold and aim. | 1. Relax fingers of bow hand; use a bow sling. |
| 2. Fingers are extended and locked into position. | 2. Relax fingers of bow hand. Though this technique can appear to keep hand from gripping bow, it puts tension in bow hand, and you may grab bow at release anyway. |
| 3. Wrist slides around to right or left on handle. | 3. Place your hand so the center line of your arm intersects the center of the bow. |
| 4. Face of bow turns to right or left during draw. | 4. Center your hand behind the bow, and relax your fingers. |
| 5. Arrows occasionally land right or left of the bull's-eye when aimed at the bull's-eye. | 5. Relax your bow hand so you're not gripping the bow. Use a bow sling. Make sure your bow hand is not too far right or too far left on the bow handle. |
| 6. Arrows land high on the target. | 6. Avoid pushing on your bow with the heel of your bow hand at release. |
| **Anchor Position** | |
| 1. Draw hand comes away from the head on release (plucks string). | 1. Make sure the force for your draw comes from your back muscles and that the draw hand remains relaxed throughout. Check for indications that your hand is tense, such as flexed base knuckles or wrist; relax your hand and wrist if they are tense. |
| 2. Draw hand fails to follow through (dead release). | 2. Release string by relaxing your hand rather than forcing your fingers open. |
| 3. The three fingers come off the bowstring at slightly different times at release. | 3. Release string by relaxing your hand rather than forcing your fingers open; all three fingers should come off the string at the same time. |
| 4. The bowstring is crooked (torqued) because of the way the draw hand is oriented at full draw. | 4. Make sure the back of your draw hand is perpendicular to the ground, not palm down. |
| 5. Under-chin anchor floats beneath chin. | 5. Feel your hand on your chin. |
| 6. Release aid is "punched" (a jerky, forward movement). | 6. Increase back tension throughout aim; trigger slowly so that release is a surprise and not anticipated. |

# DRILLS

### 1. Impact Variation Drill

This drill demonstrates how stance influences your sight setting. Shoot an end from 20 yards to make sure you are sighted in to the bull's eye. Now shoot an end with a square stance. Note the center of your arrow group; estimate and record the distance of your arrow group from the bull's-eye in the following section. Now shoot an end with a closed stance. Again note the center of your arrow group. Shoot a final end with an open stance, and note the center of your arrow group.

**Success Goal** = See the effect of varying the stance ____

____inches from bull's-eye, square stance ____

____inches from bull's-eye, closed stance ____

____inches from bull's-eye, open stance ____

**Success Check**
• Body erect ____
• Weight even ____

### 2. Golf Tee Drill

With two golf tees in hand, take a stance on the shooting line. Push the golf tees into the ground at your toes. Now move behind the shooting line. Sight down the golf tees to see whether an imaginary line through your stance goes straight to the target. Record whether this line intersects the bull's eye. Repeat this exercise by moving several steps up the shooting line and then several steps down the line from your first position. Often three or four archers shoot at a target at one time. You must learn to take a correct stance even if you cannot stand squarely in front of the target.

**Success Goal** = 3 repetitions with perfect alignment ____

**Success Check**
• Feet shoulder-width apart ____
• Square shoulders to target ____

### 3. Partner Stance Check

Choose a partner. Take your natural stance in front of the target from about 20 yards distance. Shoot an arrow. Have your partner stand behind you, looking down the range, and sight down the imaginary line that would intersect your front and back shoulder to see whether it points to the bull's eye as you come to full draw. Shoot arrows from different positions along the shooting line. Have your partner check you each time.

**Success Goal** = 3 repetitions with perfect alignment ___

✔ *Success Check*
• Line up on imaginary line to target ___
• Assume your chosen stance exactly ___

## 4. Distance Drill

Variations in your stance affect your accuracy more at longer distances. Shoot four ends of six arrows at each distance of 20, 25, 30, and 35 yards at an 80 centimeter target. Use golf tees to maintain a consistent stance at each distance. Plot the 24 arrows shot at each distance with an X on the charts below. Look for any horizontal drift in your groups as you increase shooting distance.

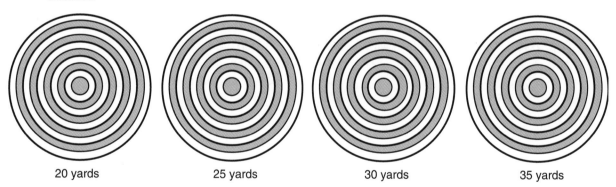

| 20 yards | 25 yards | 30 yards | 35 yards |

**Success Goal** = Maintain centering of groups at increasing distance ___

20 yards: Drift? _____

25 yards: Drift? _____

30 yards: Drift? _____

35 yards: Drift? _____

✔ **Success Check**
✔ **Success Check**
• Replicate stance at each distance ____
• Square shoulders ____

**To Increase Difficulty**
• Move in 10-yard increments.

**To Decrease Difficulty**
• Use a larger target.
• If you find that your arrows drift with increasing distance, use the golf tees as in drill 2 whenever you shoot from various distances until you can line up with the target perfectly at any distance, in any position.

## 5. Choosing a Bow Hand Position

Shoot two ends of six arrows each from 20 yards with a high wrist. Now do the same with a straight wrist and then with a low wrist. Changing your bow hand position is likely to move the impact point of your arrows from the bull's eye. Do not be concerned with the location of your group right now, but note in the following section how tight the group was and how comfortable the position was by writing *good* or *poor* in the appropriate space. The position that produces the tightest groups and is the most comfortable one for you is the one you should use. Make sure the center line of the arm intersects the center of the bow (see figure below).

((( **Success Goal** = Establish the bow hand position that is the most comfortable and produces the tightest groups ____

High wrist:     End 1 Comfort _____ Group _____
                End 2 Comfort _____ Group _____
Straight wrist: End 1 Comfort _____ Group _____
                End 2 Comfort _____ Group _____
Low wrist:      End 1 Comfort _____ Group _____
                End 2 Comfort _____ Group _____

Position chosen: _____

✔ **Success Check**
• Center line of arm intersects center of bow ____
• Relax hand and fingers ____

## 6. Torque Check

Without an arrow, take your stance and grip your bow as usual while an observer watches from a few feet down range. As you draw the string back, the observer should note whether the back of the bow always faces the target or turns to the right or left. The observer can also watch a stabilizer or extended sight if you have one of these on your bow to see whether it points right or left during the draw. If the bow turns right or left, change your hand position on the handle until you can draw without torquing the bow.

**Success Goal** = 5 successive draws without torquing the bow ___

**Success Check**
• Draw straight back ___
• Draw close to bow arm ___

## 7. Consistency Check

Obtain two small pieces of tape or two dot stickers. Place one on the middle of the bow handle just above where you place your hand. Take your bow hand position and place the second sticker on your hand right below the other dot on the bow. Shoot two ends. Before drawing for each shot, take your bow hand position, and check to see whether the stickers or pieces of tape are aligned.

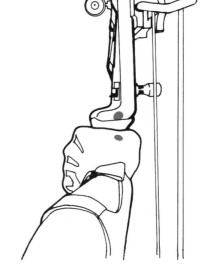

**Success Goal** = 10 of 12 shots in alignment ___

**Success Check**

• Center line of arm intersects center of bow ___

## 8. Distance Practice

Bow hand errors become more obvious as you increase your distance from the target. Shoot three ends of six arrows at 20 yards, three ends at 30 yards, and then three ends at 40 yards. For each distance, plot your arrows on the targets below. Note your directional errors. Also, note whether the amount of error increased as the distance increased by writing *same* or *more*. Check the Success Stoppers. Note whether your directional errors could be related to a flaw in bow hand technique.

**Success Goal** = Accurate ends despite increasing shooting distance ___

20 yards: Direction _____ Amount _____

30 yards: Direction _____ Amount _____

40 yards: Direction _____ Amount _____

Possible flaw in bow hand position:

_____

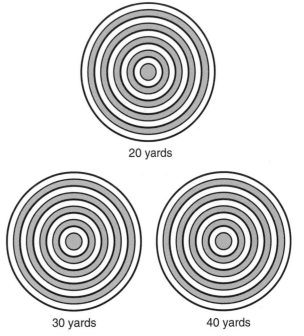

20 yards

30 yards          40 yards

### ✔ *Success Check*
- Increase back tension while aiming ___
- Relax hand and fingers ___

### *To Decrease Difficulty*
- If you used a high or straight wrist for this drill and found that you could not maintain your bow hand position as you shot more and more arrows, consider using a low wrist position.

## 9. Relaxation Check

Extend your bow arm. Relax your wrist; if it is relaxed, it should droop toward the ground. Take your string hand and hook the skin web between the thumb and forefinger of your bow hand. This action mimics the pressure of the bow when it is drawn. Hold this position for a count of three, and try to maintain a relaxed wrist and hand. When you let go with your draw hand, your bow hand should fall into its original drooped position. If it remains up, you have let tension develop in your wrist. Repeat this drill 12 times.

### ⟨⟨ *Success Goal* = 10 of 12 repetitions with a relaxed wrist ___

### ✔ *Success Check*
- Relax hand ___
- Relax fingers ___

## 10. Mimic With Eyes Closed

Take only your bow and assume your stance, bow hand hold, and hook. Raise the bow and draw to an under-chin anchor with your eyes closed. Feel for the proper position, hold for a count of three while maintaining relaxed hands, and then ease the string back. This drill establishes your feel for proper anchor position. Repeat the drill with two other anchor positions.

### ⟨⟨ *Success Goal* = 10 successive repetitions with each anchor position ___

Under-chin anchor ___

_____ anchor ___

_____ anchor ___

### ✔ *Success Check*
- Touch string to nose ___
- Hand close to neck ___

## 11. Setting the Kisser Button

In previous drills, you tried the various anchor positions. Decide which one you will use for the near future. You can now install a kisser button for this anchor position. Slip the kisser button onto the string above the nock locator. Now take a normal stance and draw to your anchor. Note whether you feel the kisser button above or below your lips. Let down and adjust the kisser button in the direction of your lips. Repeat this process until the button is between your lips. Mark this location on the bowstring. If you are using personal equipment, attach the button to the string with an open ring that you clamp down with nocking pliers.

**Success Goal** = Correctly position the kisser button ____

Height of kisser button above nock locator:

_____

**To Decrease Difficulty**
- Have a partner move the button to the proper location while you hold at full draw.

**Success Check**
- Kisser button touches between lips ____

## 12. Sight Setting

If you are now using a new anchor position you need to re-establish your sight settings. Also, if you have made a slight change in your under-chin anchor, you need to check your sight settings. Start at 10 yards. Shoot until you obtain an accurate sight setting. Move back to 15 yards, and then move back to 20, 25, 30, 35, and 40 yards, shooting until you have an accurate sight setting. If you are using a new anchor, there is likely to be more difference in your setting at a longer distance than a shorter distance.

**Success Goal** = Obtain an accurate sight setting at each distance ____

Sight settings: ____10 yards

____15 yards

____20 yards

____25 yards

____30 yards

____35 yards

____40 yards

**Success Check**
- Touch kisser button ____
- Establish touch points ____
- Center target and sight in peep sight ____

**To Increase Difficulty**
- Add 45- and 50-yard settings.

**To Decrease Difficulty**
- Start at 10 yards and stop at 30 yards.

## 13. Scoring Drill

Now that you have had a chance to perfect one of the anchor positions, check your success in scoring well. Start at 40 yards on an 80 centimeter target face and shoot four ends of six arrows each. Repeat this drill at 30 and 20 yards.

**Success Goal** = Improve your score as you move closer to the target ____

| 40 yards | End 1 ____ points |
| | End 2 ____ points |
| | End 3 ____ points |
| | End 4 ____ points |
| | Total ____ points |
| 30 yards | End 1 ____ points |
| | End 2 ____ points |
| | End 3 ____ points |
| | End 4 ____ points |
| | Total ____ points |
| 20 yards | End 1 ____ points |
| | End 2 ____ points |
| | End 3 ____ points |
| | End 4 ____ points |
| | Total ____ points |

**Success Check**
- Draw elbow back ____
- Draw straight back ____
- Establish touch points ____
- Relax hand ____

**To Increase Difficulty**
- Add 35 and 25 yards.

**To Decrease Difficulty**
- Shoot at 30, 25, and 20 yards.
- Use a larger target.

## SHOT REFINEMENT SUCCESS SUMMARY

You now have developed a personal shooting style by deciding which variation of stance, bow hand position, and anchor to use. Have a teacher or observer compare your technique to the appropriate Keys to Success checklist from figures 5.1 through 5.3. By perfecting these three parts of your shot, you have adapted your shooting technique to your individual body shape and structure and the type of archery you want to pursue.

# STEP

# 6 TROUBLESHOOTING: ANALYZING YOUR OWN PERFORMANCE

S ome of the most famous people in sports are coaches: Don Shula in football, Tommy Lasorda in baseball, Pat Summitt in basketball. Such coaches are known for their success in helping their athletes reach their full potential. Like any other athletes, archers also benefit from coaching. An archery coach can note flaws in shooting technique and suggest a correction. Unfortunately, archery coaches are not as plentiful as basketball and baseball coaches. Yet archers can learn to detect and correct their own errors.

Archers rely on two sources of information to correct performance mistakes. They analyze where their arrows land in relation to the bull's-eye where their shots are aimed. They also check their technique by evaluating the feel of their shot or watching a videotape. Successful archers, no matter what type of archery they shoot, learn how to check their own shooting and make adjustments in their technique. The technology available today even makes this evaluation fun!

## Why Is Troubleshooting Important?

Any archer would probably seize the opportunity to work with a good coach. Even archers lucky enough to have a coach, though, spend many hours shooting without the coach when practicing, competing, or hunting. The sooner an error can be corrected, the better. Remember that most types of archery involve repetitive shooting. Archers who can quickly adjust their technique to overcome mistakes will score more consistently than those who cannot.

## Monitoring Performance

There are two basic methods of monitoring any errors that develop in your shooting. One way is to observe the result of your performance. In archery, this method involves an analysis of the pattern your arrows form on the target face. Form errors can cause consistent directional errors. For example, if several arrows in each of your ends land to the right of your other arrows, several shooting flaws are the likely cause. If all your arrows land to the right of the bull's-eye, despite repeated corrections of your sight setting, you can pinpoint one of these shooting flaws as the cause. The second method for checking performance is to observe your technique. In archery, you observe your stance, draw, anchor, hold, release, and follow-through for alignment, consistency, and proper execution.

### Arrow Pattern Analysis

Your arrows land in the bull's eye if they are both vertically and horizontally accurate. Technique errors made repetitively result in a consistent directional error. You can identify the error or flaw by checking the pattern of the arrows on the target face.

To help describe shot locations, the target face is often compared to a clock face as you view it from the shooting line. Arrows landing to the right of the bull's-eye, for example, are described as three o'clock errors. Arrows landing right and slightly high are called two o'clock errors, and so on. Consistent directional errors also can be related to your equipment. Later, you will learn how to adjust your equipment in order to eliminate directional errors due to your equipment setup.

## Horizontal Patterns

The performance errors that affect horizontal accuracy generally include horizontal movements of the bow or bow arm, misalignment of the bowstring and bowsight, misalignment in addressing the target, and releases that give the bowstring too much horizontal movement (see figure 6.1a-d). Horizontal bow movements can occur if you do the following:

■ Cant (tilt) your bow

■ Move the bow to the right or left when you release the bowstring

■ Allow your bow arm wrist to break upon release

■ Hold the bow handle to the side

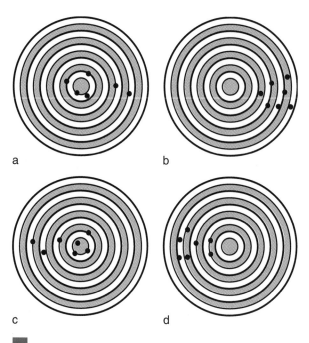

**Figure 6.1** Horizontal bow movements.

Many archers are so anxious to see their arrow hit the target that they move the bow sideways upon release. To prevent yourself from making this mistake, make sure you do the following:

■ Use your back muscles to draw

■ Keep your arms in alignment with the target

■ Center your bow arm behind the center of the bow handle

■ Follow through in T-form

Misalignments of the bowstring and bowsight often result from the following actions:

■ Varying the anchor position

■ Changing the eye that aligns the bowstring and bowsight from shot to shot

■ Varying the pattern of alignment between the bowstring and the bowsight from shot to shot

Because the arrow is snapped onto the bowstring, changing the position of the bowstring in relation to the aiming aperture changes the orientation of the arrow to the bull's-eye from shot to shot. You can avoid these misalignments by doing the following:

■ Using a consistent anchor

■ Using at least the tip of the nose as a touch point for the bowstring

■ Establishing a consistent bowstring/bowsight pattern from shot to shot

The preferred bowstring/bowsight pattern is to place the string just to the right of the aiming aperture. A peep sight automatically gives you a consistent pattern, but it is prohibited in some competition classifications.

Misalignments in addressing the target usually affect the accuracy of the shot because muscles on one side of the body are working harder than those on the other side. The tensed muscles tend to cause horizontal movements upon release, especially as you tire. Remember to do the following when addressing the target:

■ Establish a solid base of support with your stance without using a very open or closed position

■ Keep the body aligned to the target by drawing close to the bow arm with the back muscles

■ Avoid bows with a draw weight so heavy that you need additional movements to get to full draw

Releases that give the bowstring unnecessary horizontal movement affect accuracy because they send the tail of the arrow farther to the side than is necessary. Remember that the arrow remains in contact with the bowstring for most of its path forward. The release most likely to cause horizontal errors is plucking the string, which means the hand flies away from the face rather than recoiling over the rear shoulder. Arrow flight also is affected if you nock the arrow backwards so that the index feather strikes the arrow rest or bow window or if the bowstring catches on clothing or jewelry as it moves forward.

## Vertical Patterns

The performance errors that affect vertical accuracy include the following:

- Moving your bow arm up or down upon release
- Varying your anchor position vertically
- Varying the pressure of the fingers on the bowstring
- Holding the bow too high or low on the handle
- Varying from T-form
- Varying your effective draw length (see figure 6.2a-d)

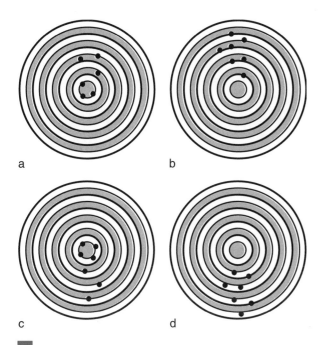

a          b

c          d

**Figure 6.2**   Vertical bow movements.

Dropping or raising the bow arm on release can affect the tail end of the arrow as it clears the bow. Always follow through by slightly pushing the bow arm to the bull's-eye until the arrow hits the target.

Varying the anchor position vertically orients the arrow differently from shot to shot. Beginning archers often anchor with their mouths open and vary how wide their mouths are open with each shot. Avoid this error by keeping your teeth together on every shot. Varying the pressure of the three fingers on the bowstring also changes the orientation of the arrow. Releases that cause vertical errors are those in which the wrist rotates up or down so that the pressure of the upper or lower finger lessens just before release.

Holding the bow at the same location on the handle on every shot minimizes vertical errors. Holding the handle too high or too low is likely to cause you to move the bow when you release the bowstring. For example, you could heel the bow with the base of the palm and tilt the bow backwards as a result.

Varying from T-form can also contribute to vertical errors, especially if you do the following:

- Hunch the front shoulder
- Slide the hips forward
- Tilt the head forward or back
- Lean forward or back

These form errors contribute to vertical bow arm movement and variation in the effective draw length. Even small variations in draw length can affect vertical accuracy by changing the pounds of thrust imparted to the arrow. The following movements and variations cause arrows to land at six o'clock:

- Moving the draw hand slightly forward at release (creeping)
- Bending the bow arm
- Tilting the head forward
- Punching (moving forward) when triggering a mechanical release

Maintaining T-form and using the back muscles to draw prevents these variations. Increasing the back tension during the aim, and then releasing the bowstring by relaxing the fingers, produces the most consistent draw and release.

## Mixed Patterns

Several situations could result in arrow patterns of mixed vertical and horizontal errors, such as ten o'clock or four o'clock errors. An archer may make multiple errors, some causing vertical errors and some causing horizontal errors. Such a pattern also results from moving the bow arm diagonally rather than just vertically or horizontally. If your arrows form a mixed pattern, make sure you maintain a loose grip on the bow and push the bow arm straight to the bull's-eye throughout the aim, release, and follow-through. If your arrows still form a mixed pattern, look for errors that effect both horizontal and vertical accuracy. For example, if your arrows land at four or five o'clock, look for errors that cause a right, horizontal error and a low, vertical error.

## Technique Analysis

You can identify technique errors in your shooting by examining videotapes or pictures of yourself or using a friend as an observer. Watch carefully for T-form in back and front views. Watch for alignment along a line straight to the target in views from behind, looking down range. You also may be able to feel yourself making a technique error, although archers often do not realize how they are positioning their bodies and limbs.

### Techniques Affecting Horizontal Accuracy

Many technique errors that cause horizontal errors are detected from a camera view or observer angle behind the archer, viewing down range (see figure 6.3a). From this angle, check for positions or movements that cause horizontal variations in arrow flight:

- The body leaning right or left, perhaps falling off that direction upon release
- The shoulders are angled down range

- The bow arm appearing to the right or left from behind the trunk upon release
- The bow tilting right or left
- The bow turning right or left upon release
- The string hand or arm flying away from the face upon release

Sometimes a rear view from a location above the archer is helpful in detecting these technique flaws (see figures 6.3 b and c). Extend your tripod or have your observer stand carefully on a ladder. A few aspects of form that affect horizontal accuracy can be observed by a close-up of the face and draw hand. Watch for slight variations in establishing the anchor position, such as touching the bowstring to the tip of the nose on one shot but the side of the nose on another. If an observer sees these positions or movements, or you see them on videotape, note the Keys to Success in figure 6.3.

---

**FIGURE 6.3** **KEYS TO SUCCESS**

# HORIZONTAL ACCURACY

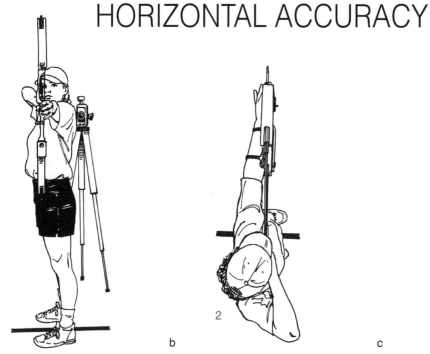

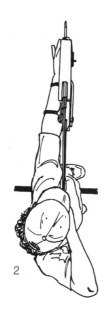

a

1. Release bowstring cleanly ___

b

2. Align the shoulder toward target ___
3. Use a consistent anchor position ___

c

4. Align the bow vertically ___
5. Adjust equipment for clean arrow clearance of bow ___

### Techniques Affecting Vertical Accuracy

Technique errors that cause vertical errors are most often detected from an observer or camera position down the shooting line, directed toward the front of the body (see figure 6.4a). From this perspective, check for these positions or movements that cause vertical variations in arrow flight:

- An uneven shoulder line
- The body leaning toward or away from the target
- The hips sliding forward and the upper body tilting back

- The bow arm moving up or down upon release
- Shot to shot variations in the anchor position
- Shot to shot variations in the bow hand grip
- Shot to shot variations in finger pressure

Zoom in on the string or bow hand to see whether its position varies from shot to shot (see figure 6.4b). An observer also can stand behind you as you're shooting to observe your form by looking at your back (see figure 6.4c). If you or an observer notes that you are using the positions, movements, or variations in the preceding list, review the Keys to Success in figure 6.4.

**FIGURE 6.4** | KEYS TO SUCCESS

## VERTICAL ACCURACY

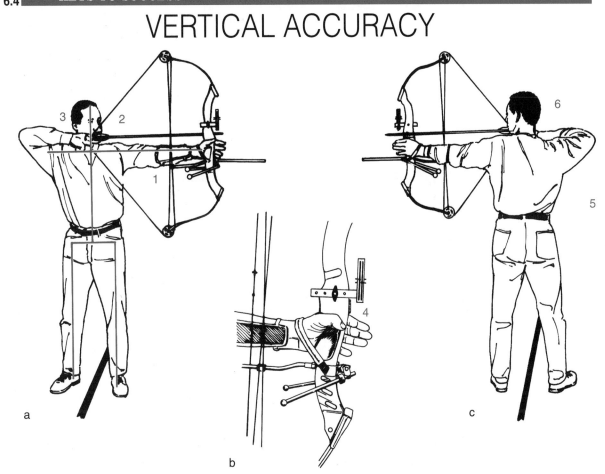

1. Keep the bow arm up ___
2. Keep finger pressure on bowstring even ___
3. Use a consistent anchor ___

4. Use a consistent bow hand grip ___
5. Stand upright ___
6. Keep draw length consistent from shot to shot ___

## TROUBLESHOOTING SUCCESS STOPPERS

Analyzing your arrow patterns and your shooting technique should be an ongoing activity. The sooner you can detect and correct errors the less likely they are to become bad habits.

| Error | Correction |
|---|---|
| 1. Your bow arm moves up, down, or sideways on release. | 1. Resist the weight of the draw by slightly pushing the bow arm toward the bull's-eye during the draw and aim and after the release.<br><br>**Explanation:** Although this movement may at first occur after the shot, the tendency over time is for archers to move sooner and sooner so that eventually the bow contacts the tail end of the arrow and sends it off line. |
| 2. You torque the bow on release. | 2. Develop a relaxed bow hand; see the drills in step 5.<br><br>**Explanation:** When the bow hand grip is tight, archers tend to flex the finger upon release, an action that turns the bow handle. With a relaxed bow hand grip, the bow is free to jump slightly forward upon release and not affect the arrow either horizontally or vertically. Using a bow sling helps to prevent archers from feeling that they have to hold the bow so that it will not fall. |
| 3. You torque the bowstring. | 3. Use the back muscles to draw, increase back tension during aim, and keep both hands relaxed. |
| 4. You come out of T-form during the draw, aim, or follow-through. | 4. Use a bow with a draw weight that you can control without losing T-form; draw using the back muscles; avoid an extremely open or closed stance.<br><br>**Explanation:** Many T-form flaws are the result of archers shooting a bow too high in draw weight. They cannot draw with just the back muscles so they recruit other muscle groups. Rather than maintaining alignment of the limbs and trunk, they move the arm, shoulder, and trunk joints. |
| 5. You release the bowstring when the bowsight is directed outside the bull's-eye. | 5. Develop the habit of settling on the bull's-eye for several seconds before releasing the bowstring. If problems persist, use a draw check. |
| 6. Your alignment varies from shot to shot. | 6. Use a consistent anchor position; align the string and bowsight consistently or use a peep sight if rules allow. |

# DRILLS

## 1. Checking Vertical Alignment Errors

Place a camcorder on a tripod about chest high and 10 feet up the shooting line from your shooting position so that the recording provides the view in figure a. If possible, suspend a sheet or canvas with vertical and horizontal lines from a coat rack behind you. Record at least 10 shots. If you do not have access to a camcorder, have a friend take still photographs or observe your shooting. Watch the videotape and look for body alignment errors such as those shown in figures b and c. Compare your alignment to the vertical and horizontal lines on the sheet. Try to correct any alignment errors as you videotape five additional shots. Repeat this cycle until you shoot with good alignment.

a

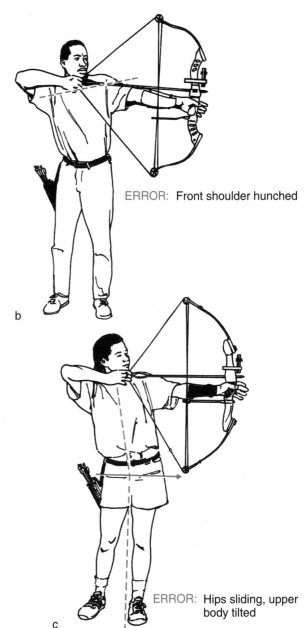

ERROR: Front shoulder hunched

b

ERROR: Hips sliding, upper body tilted

c

**Success Goal** = Correct alignment errors after analyzing 15 shots ___

✔ **Success Check**
• Keep shoulders level ___
• Stand erect ___
• Keep bow arm up ___

**To Increase Difficulty**
• Videotape the last 10 shots of a 60-shot practice session. Remember that form tends to break down as you tire, yet the last arrow counts just as much as the first arrow in competition.

## 2. Checking Horizontal Alignment Errors

Place a camcorder or observer behind you, looking down range. Shoot 10 arrows, and then check with your observer or watch the videotape. Try to detect alignment errors that would affect the arrow horizontally, such as an uneven stance or incorrect T-form. Now try to correct those errors as you videotape five additional shots. Repeat this cycle until you shoot with good alignment.

a

ERROR: Upper body bent

b

ERROR: Stance misaligned

c

ERROR: Shoulders not aligned to target

**Success Goal** = Correct alignment errors after analyzing 15 shots ___

**Success Check**
- Align stance and shoulders toward target ___
- Maintain T-form by drawing with back muscles ___
- Stand erect ___

**To Increase Difficulty**
- Videotape the last 10 shots of a 60-shot practice session.

## 3. Checking Anchor Variations

Videotape 10 shots as in drill 1, except zoom in or move the tripod to record a close-up view of your anchor position and release. Watch the videotape to detect incorrect anchor positions or variations in your anchor position from shot to shot. Look especially for the flaws shown in figures a, b, and c. If you find errors in your anchor position, review step 5. If you find variations in your anchor position, develop a mental checklist to remind yourself to position your anchor consistently. Now videotape 10 additional shots to see whether you are more consistent.

a
ERROR: Mouth open,
anchor lowered

b
ERROR: String drawn
past nose

c
ERROR: Head rotated

**Success Goal** = Position your anchor consistently for 10 shots ___

**To Increase Difficulty**
• Record your anchor position for 30 shots.

**Success Check**
• Touch string to nose ___

## 4. Checking Release Errors

Use your videotape or pictures from drill 3, but examine your release. Compare the ideal of relaxing the string fingers (or triggering your mechanical release) and the hand following through over the rear shoulder. Errors might involve the fingers, hand, or elbow of the string arm.

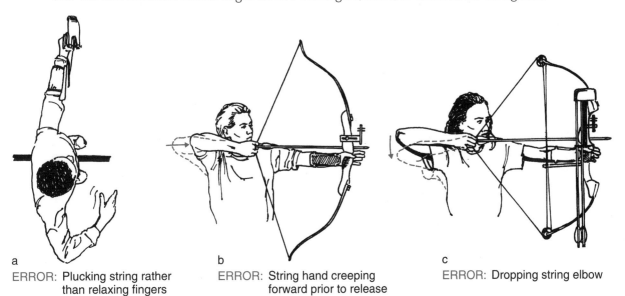

a
ERROR: Plucking string rather
than relaxing fingers

b
ERROR: String hand creeping
forward prior to release

c
ERROR: Dropping string elbow

**Success Goal** = Execute 10 shots with a perfect release ___

**To Increase Difficulty**
• Record your release for 30 shots.

**Success Check**
• Increase back tension ___
• Relax fingers ___

## 5. Checking Bow Hand Errors

Videotape 10 shots as in drill 1, except zoom in or move the tripod to record your bow hand, or work with a partner. Watch the videotape or consult with your partner. The bow should jump forward slightly upon release, and the fingers should remain relaxed. If you find that you grab the bow, heel it, or turn it upon release, as shown in figures a, b, and c, review step 5 to work on a relaxed bow hand. Also, watch the time period before release to assure that your wrist position does not change during the draw and aim. Record 10 additional shots to monitor your improvement.

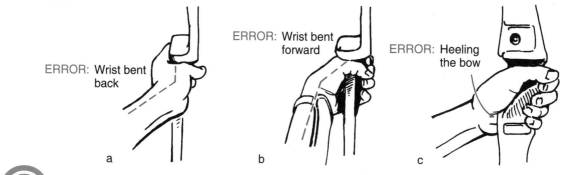

a  b  c

**Success Goal** = Execute 10 shots with a relaxed bow hand ___

**To Increase Difficulty**
• Record the last 10 shots of a 60-shot practice session.

**Success Check**
• Bow arm and hand aligned behind handle ___
• Fingers relaxed ___

## 6. Checking Draw Errors

Videotape 10 shots as in drill 1 and then watch the videotape, or work with a partner. Analyze your draw. Identify errors such as those pictured in figures a and b. Ideally, your bow arm is extended throughout the draw, and your draw comes all the way to your anchor position. After you identify any draw errors, videotape 10 additional shots and analyze them. Repeat this cycle until you eliminate your errors.

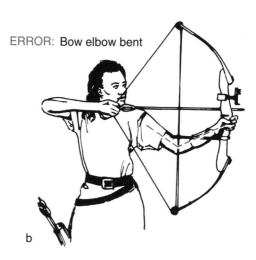

a  b

**Success Goal** = 10 shots with a perfect draw ___

**✔ Success Check**
• Extend bow arm to target ___
• Touch string to nose ___

**■ To Increase Difficulty**
• Record the last 10 shots of a 60-shot practice session.

## 7. Checking Follow-Through

Videotape 10 shots as in drill 1 and then watch the videotape, or work with a partner. Analyze your follow-through. Identify errors such as those pictured in figures a, b, and c. Ideally, your bow arm is extended throughout the draw and follow-through. When you release the bowstring, your head and bow arm should maintain their position, keeping T-form. After you identify any follow-through errors, videotape 10 additional shots and analyze them. Repeat this cycle until you eliminate your errors.

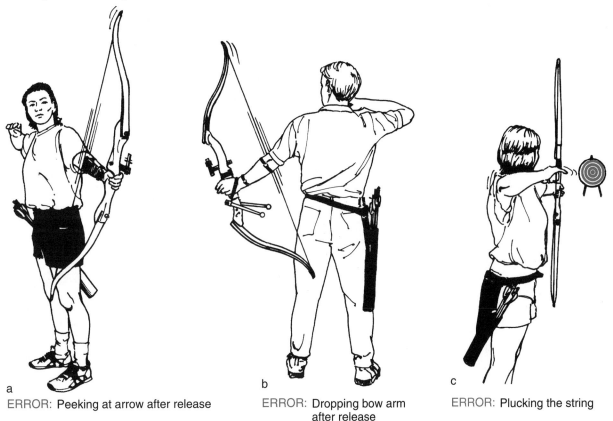

a
ERROR: Peeking at arrow after release

b
ERROR: Dropping bow arm after release

c
ERROR: Plucking the string

**Success Goal** = 10 shots with a perfect follow-through ___

**✔ Success Check**
• Maintain head position upon release ___
• Bow arm extends to target even after release ___

**■ To Increase Difficulty**
• Record the last 10 shots of a 60-shot practice session.

## 8. Checking Aiming Errors

Aiming errors are difficult to detect by observation. Another method of detecting errors is needed. The following list of items could comprise your mental checklist for aiming. Shoot an arrow, and then look down the list. Did you forget any items? Continue shooting until you can execute an entire end without forgetting a step.

**Success Goal** = Remember the following steps on every shot ___

1. Close your dominant eye if it's not on the same side as your string hand.
2. Line up the bowstring just to the right of the aiming aperture (or center aiming aperture in peep sight).
3. See the bowstring bisect the bow limbs in your peripheral vision (or check the bubble in the level).
4. Exhale before aiming and releasing.
5. Let the bowsight settle in the bull's eye before you release the bowstring. Note that the sight doesn't have to stop dead in the bull's eye.

**Success Check**
- Establish consistent string/sight pattern ___
- Allow sight to settle in bull's eye before release ___

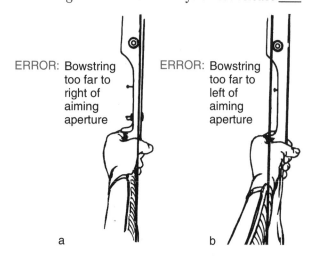

ERROR: Bowstring too far to right of aiming aperture

ERROR: Bowstring too far to left of aiming aperture

a                          b

## 9. Arrow Pattern Analysis

Shoot several ends from 20 yards. Before pulling your arrows, plot each arrow's location with an X on the targets provided. When you finish, look for your most common directional errors. Record whether your arrow pattern reflects horizontal errors, vertical errors, or both. Then identify several potential causes of your errors. Shoot several more ends, and try to avoid the errors you identified. Plot these ends on additional targets to see whether you have eliminated or reduced directional error.

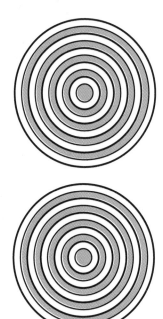

**Success Goal** = Correct the identified directional errors ____

Are your errors

____ vertical?

____ horizontal?

Possible Causes

1._____

2._____

3._____

4._____

5._____

**Success Check**
- Maintain T-form ____
- Establish consistent bow hand and anchor positions ____
- Follow through to target ____

## 10. Distance Arrow Pattern Analysis

Directional errors often become more noticeable as you shoot from longer distances. Once directed off center, the arrow continues over a longer distance on a line that results in its landing farther from the bull's-eye. Shoot several ends from 30 yards. Before pulling your arrows, plot each arrow's location with an X on the targets provided with this drill. When you finish shooting and plotting, look for your most common directional errors. Record whether your arrow pattern reflects horizontal errors, vertical errors, or both. Then identify several potential causes of your errors. Shoot several more ends, and try to avoid the errors you identified. Plot these ends on additional targets to see whether you have eliminated or reduced directional error.

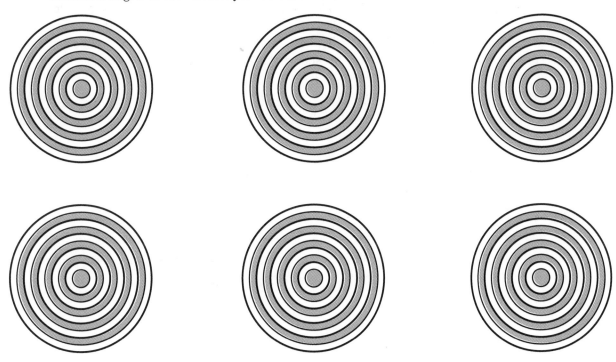

**Success Goal** = Correct the identified directional errors ___

Are your errors

_____ vertical?

_____ horizontal?

Possible Causes

1._____

2._____

3._____

4._____

5._____

**Success Check**

• Maintain T-form ___
• Establish consistent bow hand and anchor positions ___
• Follow through to target ___

## TROUBLESHOOTING SUCCESS SUMMARY

Technique errors affect horizontal accuracy, vertical accuracy, or both. You can avoid horizontal deviations in your shots (also called three o'clock and nine o'clock errors) by maintaining bow and string alignment. You can avoid vertical deviations in your shots (also called twelve o'clock and six o'clock errors) by keeping T-form, keeping your draw length consistent, and following through. Diagonal errors, such as eight o'clock or four o'clock errors, can indicate that you are making multiple technique errors that are affecting both horizontal and vertical accuracy. Remember to repeat the drills in this step periodically. Ask a friend or practice partner to assess your troubleshooting abilities by using the Keys to Success in figures 6.3 and 6.4. Detecting and correcting your errors early can minimize the chance that they will become bad habits.

### Summary Comparison Chart

| Causes of horizontal (three o'clock and nine o'clock) errors: | Causes for six o'clock errors: |
|---|---|
| • Canting the bow | • Dropping bow arm |
| • Moving the bow sideways on release | • Creeping |
| • Breaking your bow wrist on release | • Not coming to full draw |
| • Holding the bow to the side of handle center | **Causes for twelve o'clock errors:** |
| • Misaligning the bowstring with the sight aperture | • Raising bow arm upon release |
| • Taking a stance that is not aligned to the target | • Opening mouth and therefore lowering your anchor |
| | • Overdrawing |

# STEP

# 7

# PUTTING IT TOGETHER: DEVELOPING A POSITIVE MENTAL OUTLOOK

You have heard athletes from many different sports talk about performing "in the zone." They are referring to a time or contest when their performance was superior, and success came almost without thought and effort. Their concentration was extremely focused, even to the point that objects appeared larger than normal or actions seemed as if they were in slow motion. Experiencing the zone while shooting archery is truly incredible! The bull's-eye seems so large it is hard to miss. The bow feels light. Drawing the bow is effortless.

Performance in the zone is rare. Most athletes would be fortunate to experience it once in their careers. Athletes cannot make themselves perform in the zone, but they can prepare themselves mentally as well as physically to perform. With good mental preparation, athletes open the door for superior performance. They create the conditions that almost always result in success and occasionally result in a once-in-a-lifetime performance. In this step, you will learn how to take a positive mental approach to shooting archery.

## Why Create a Mental Checklist?

A mental checklist is a helpful way to proceed through shot setup. It reminds you to attend to the necessary aspects of shot preparation and leaves you little time

to think about other things or about being nervous. If you tend to repeat the same form error, a checklist can include a specific reminder to avoid the error. A mental checklist helps you methodically and precisely prepare every shot in the same way. Your checklist points can vary on a daily basis with shooting conditions. For example, an archer shooting at a target on a sloping hillside often unwittingly cants the bow. The addition of a mental checklist reminder to level the bow helps the archer check for a level bow on each and every shot.

## How to Develop a Personal Checklist

Begin the development of your personal checklist by identifying the Keys to Success pertinent to your shooting style. Figure 7.1 gives a skeleton list of the Keys to Success. Where you might have decided to use a variation in your shot setup, a blank is left for you to fill in an appropriate cue.

A mental checklist is highly personalized. It can reflect your unique shooting style and address the bad habits into which you tend to fall. With practice, you can streamline your checklist. The Mental Checklist Keys to Success assume that some of the simplest aspects of shooting are now habitual and need not be specified. Feel free to add anything you tend to overlook or do incorrectly.

**FIGURE 7.1**

## KEYS TO SUCCESS
# DEVELOPING A MENTAL CHECKLIST

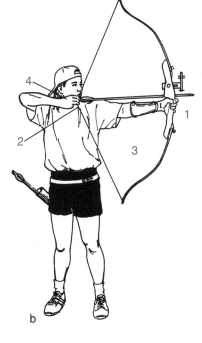

### Stance

1. Assume stance: _____
2. Nock arrow ____

### Draw and Aim

1. Set bow hand: _____
2. Set draw hand hook ____
3. Raise bow and draw ____
4. Anchor: _____
5. Align sight and level bow ____
6. Establish string pattern and sight picture ____
7. Focus, steady, and aim ____

### Release and Follow-Through

1. Tighten back muscles ____
2. Relax draw hand to release ____
3. Keep bow arm up and steady ____

## Why Is Mental Preparation Important?

From your experience with other sports and now with archery, you can see that the movements involved in archery are relatively simple. Most participants can develop good shooting form if they have an interest in doing so. What often distinguishes elite performers from good performers is their mental approach to shooting. You can enhance your performance by learning to focus on the important aspects of shooting and blocking out unnecessary or distracting thoughts.

## How to Mentally Prepare Your Shot

Three aspects of mental preparation—concentration, relaxation, and confidence—will help you shoot successfully. Every archer can improve his or her concentration, learn to relax body areas on cue, and set reasonable goals to build confidence (see figure 7.2 a-c).

### Developing Concentration

The earlier steps to success emphasized the necessity to repeat, as exactly as possible, every aspect of putting a shot together. This repetition requires concentration. Letting the mind wander to other things and forgetting a critical aspect of shooting form causes errors. Following your mental checklist in every detail on every shot maximizes the number of good shots you make. Of course, your checklist may need updating from time to time. Yet your ability to concentrate on putting a shot together by moving through the list is related to your success. It is often said that the secret to archery is learning how to make the perfect shot and then repeating it over and over again.

It is easy to say that concentration is the key to good shooting. What is difficult is knowing which aspects of putting a shot together need your attention. This information is in part difficult because it changes as you acquire archery skill. In the early steps, you might recall that the Keys to Success contained details about preparing a shot that were later dropped. With practice, they became second nature. As archers acquire skill, they trim their checklists of items needing conscious attention to a minimum so that they can devote more of their attention to aiming.

Ideally, you should give your conscious attention on each and every shot to the items on your checklist up until the time you are ready to aim. Consider your stance, bow hand position, draw hand position, anchor, leveling, and so on. If everything feels right, aim. All of your concentration must now be devoted to aiming. Your concentration should be so intense that you seem to burn a hole in the middle of the bull's-eye. Nothing interferes with the aiming process. The physical aspects of the release are turned over to your subconscious. You must trust that if there is any indication that the shot is not right, you can assume conscious control and let the shot down. Otherwise, your subconscious will take care of making the release happen at the right time. You do not have to worry about when to make the release happen. The zone described by some athletes probably reflects their intense concentration on their goal, such as aiming at the bull's-eye in archery, and the turning over of the physical execution of their skills to their subconscious.

## Relaxing

Shooting is a rather strange mixture of tension and relaxation when compared to most sport skills. You must hold upward of 25 pounds of force while you hold the bow steady. At the same time, the very act of releasing is a relaxation, and you must maintain a completely relaxed bow hand throughout the shot, release, and follow-through. An archer must learn to be selective about which parts of the body are under tension and which are relaxed. You should practice relaxing specific parts of your body so that you can easily make your bow hand and draw hand relax at full draw.

You might find it more difficult to maintain relaxation under certain situations. Often when archers really want to shoot well, they tend to tighten their hands so that the bow sight is forced into the bull's-eye. This action is self-defeating because a tight bow hand will cause bow torque and a tight draw hand will work against a smooth release.

If you shoot archery competitively, you are likely to experience nervousness. This nervousness comes with competition in most sports. Unlike most other sports, however, you will not be moving about to relieve some of the nervous energy. In archery, you do not run, you do not hit a ball, and you do not throw a ball. Instead, you must relax and hold steady! Accept the fact that you will be nervous, but give your attention to concentrating on each and every shot. Practice relaxing on cue so that you can relax even in a competitive situation.

## Building Confidence

For an arrow to hit the center of the bull's-eye, the archer must believe it will hit the center of the bull's-eye. An archer must have confidence that every one of the arrows shot has the potential to be a bull's-eye. Remember, success in archery competition comes not from shooting one bull's-eye, but from scoring high when all the arrows that have been shot are totaled. As you perfect your form and practice, you will build confidence. You will believe that you control every shot.

What undermines confidence? A common problem with archers is trying to please others with their shooting. Many archers want to live up to someone else's expectations, even on those days when, try as one might, nothing seems to work well. The only person you need to please is yourself. If you make a mistake, don't spend your time trying to explain it away to everyone around you. Accept it, and go on.

It is easy in archery to blame the equipment for mistakes. But, if the equipment was working well last week, or a few shots ago, and you have checked to see that it is in good working order, the equipment is not to blame. Don't externalize shortcomings to the equipment. If you do, you'll cause yourself to lose confidence in being able to shoot a bull's-eye.

When archers make a mistake, they often begin to expect that they'll make that mistake again. They talk about and think about making that mistake. They undermine their confidence. If you find yourself verbalizing a negative statement about your shooting, either aloud or to yourself, turn it around to a positive statement. For example, if you find yourself saying "Oh no, it's windy, and the last time I shot in the wind I scored terribly," turn this statement around. Say, "The wind will give me a chance to improve over my last score on a windy day." You must expect that you will do well.

Some archers undermine their confidence when they set unrealistically high goals for themselves. For example, an archer who has been shooting 270 on a 300 round consistently for the last several weeks might go to a tournament wanting to shoot 280. If the 280 happens, great. But is it realistic to expect

to shoot above average in the tournament? Of course not! This archer is destined to come back from the tournament disappointed and discouraged when anything but a 280 is shot. If the goal had been to shoot 270 and that goal was achieved, the archer would be building rather than undermining confidence.

John Williams, the 1972 Olympic gold medalist, recommends setting your scoring goals conservatively. Even in practice, if you set what is really the minimum score you would ever want to shoot on a given round, your chances of feeling confident and positive after every practice session are good. Setting the minimum goal makes you work to achieve at least that level. Most often, you will score above it and in your mind you will be that many points up rather than points down. When you set a very high scoring goal and fail to reach it, you have a negative mindset, even if your score was really a very good one.

FIGURE 7.2

## KEYS TO SUCCESS

# MENTALLY PREPARING YOUR SHOT

### Stance

1. Set sight for shooting distance ___
2. Check wind ___
3. Locate target ___
4. Rehearse feeling of perfect shot ___
5. Focus attention on personal shot preparation checklist ___

### Draw and Aim

1. Continue through personal shot preparation checklist ___
2. If setup feels right, cue yourself to relax ___
3. Shift attention to aiming ___
4. Aim at bull's-eye, repeating, "Aim, aim, aim" ___

### Release and Follow-Through

1. Release explosion occurs ___
2. Maintain concentration on bull's-eye through release ___

## MENTAL SKILLS SUCCESS STOPPERS

Often an archer does not realize that negative thoughts and overt statements are replacing a positive approach to success. The following statements will encourage you to examine your thoughts and actions for evidence of a negative mindset, and then offer a suggestion for building a positive mindset.

| Error | Correction |
|---|---|
| 1. You overlook important steps in your shot preparation. | 1. Practice your mental checklist without shooting. Next, practice it while mimicking shots. Then shoot several ends with a written list, as in the Learning Your Checklist drill. |
| 2. You verbalize negative statements about your shooting. | 2. Stop the statement immediately and formulate a positive statement on same topic. Practice the Thought Stopping drill. |
| 3. You hold a visual image of a bad shot and keep seeing it over and over. | 3. Stop imagery of the bad shot; mentally rehearse a perfect shot that lands in the middle of bull's-eye. |
| 4. You consistently fail to meet scoring goals. | 4. You may be setting goals too high; consider your recent average, and then set a minimum goal slightly below this average. As you build confidence, you can raise your goals. |
| 5. You think about other things while you shoot. | 5. Practice concentrating outside of archery sessions. While shooting, focus your attention on your mental checklist. Practice the Concentration Exercise drill in this step. |
| 6. You think about form while you should be aiming. | 6. When you arrive at the aiming step in your mental checklist, shift attention completely to aiming. It may help to repeat a verbal cue to yourself over and over, such as "aim, aim, aim." Practice the Verbal Cue drill. |

## MENTAL SKILLS

# DRILLS

### 1. Learning Your Checklist

Copy the Keys to Success that you have chosen for your personal checklist onto a long, narrow sheet of paper that you can attach to the face of your upper or lower bow limb. As an alternative, copy the list with large lettering onto a large index card and lay the card on the ground in front of you (anchor it on a windy day when shooting outdoors). Use your written checklist for your next two practice sessions. Then see whether you can recite your checklist to a friend without reading it. When you can do so, shoot without the written list, but remember to mentally go through your checklist on every shot.

 **Success Goal** = Recite your checklist perfectly ___

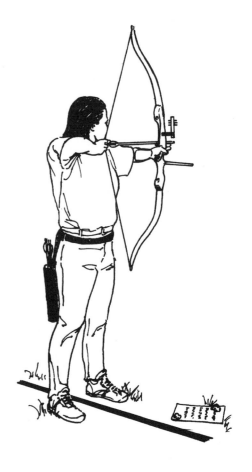

✔ **Success Check**
• Include every step ___
• Attend only to your checklist steps ___

**To Decrease Difficulty**
• Before shooting arrows, practice your mental checklist while mimicking shots.

## 2. Rehearsing Aloud

Shoot four ends at 20 yards. On each arrow, recall the items in your checklist aloud as you perform them up until you anchor. Saying the checklist aloud reminds you to attend to each item. Go through the items during the anchor and aim silently. After you release the bowstring, recall aloud your cues for maintaining follow-through.

**Success Goal** = Shoot all your arrows having executed each item in your checklist as you listed it ___

✔ **Success Check**
• Include every step ___
• Push other thoughts out of your mind ___

## 3. Balloon Practice

At this point in learning to shoot well, you need continued practice. To break the monotony of practicing on the same target face, blow up three balloons and tape them somewhere on the target face. Try to pop all three balloons in one end from a distance of 20 yards. If you don't get all three balloons in one end, continue shooting until you have popped them all. Repeat this drill at 25 yards, and then at 30 yards. Remember to use your personal checklist.

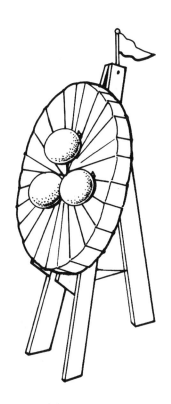

 *Success Goal* = Pop the 3 balloons in 1 end at 20 and 25 yards and in 2 ends at 30 yards ___

(#)___ ends required at 20 yards

(#)___ ends required at 25 yards

(#)___ ends required at 30 yards

✔ *Success Check*
• Attend to each step ___
• Concentrate ___

*To Increase Difficulty*
• Keep the balloons small in size.

*To Decrease Difficulty*
• Blow up the balloons to a larger size.

### 4. Tic-Tac-Toe

With a partner, obtain a two-foot-by-two-foot piece of paper or poster board. Draw a tic-tac-toe pattern on the paper and mount it on a target butt. Flip a coin to see who shoots first. You may select any shooting distance you like. Play tic-tac-toe, taking turns shooting. A shot counts if the arrow lands inside a box and does not touch any of the lines. However, you must recite your checklist during each shot, as in drill 2. If your partner catches you missing an item, you forfeit your turn. Repeat the drill as time allows.

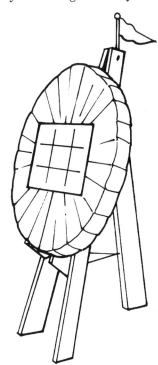

*Success Goal* = Win or draw at least half of the games played ___

_____ games won of _____ games played

✔ *Success Check*
• Recite every step ___

*To Increase Difficulty*
• Use smaller boxes for the tic-tac-toe pattern.

## 5. Subtract an Arrow

Choose a partner. Mount an 80-centimeter face on the target butt. Shoot from a mutually agreed-upon distance. Each of you should wrap a piece of tape around one of your six arrows near the fletching to mark it. Shoot your first five arrows, saving your marked arrow until last. After all 10 unmarked arrows have been shot, take turns shooting the marked arrow. You must each recite your personal checklist on this arrow. If your partner catches you leaving out an item (or vice versa), the arrow does not count in the score. If you execute your checklist successfully, the value of the marked arrow is subtracted from your partner's end score (it does not count toward your score). Repeat this drill five more times.

**Success Goal** = Win at least half of the ends ___

End 1: You ____ Partner ____

End 2: You ____ Partner ____

End 3: You ____ Partner ____

End 4: You ____ Partner ____

End 5: You ____ Partner ____

End 6: You ____ Partner ____

Wins: You ____ Partner ____

**Success Check**

• Concentrate ___
• Include every step in your checklist ___

## 6. Arrow Analysis

Shoot four ends of six arrows each from a distance of 30 yards. Plot your arrows on the target diagrams in this drill. Identify any directional errors and use the Arrow Pattern Analysis lists in step 6 (pp. 77-79) to identify the possible causes of these directional errors. Now modify your personal mental checklist to include a reminder to correct the causes of these errors.

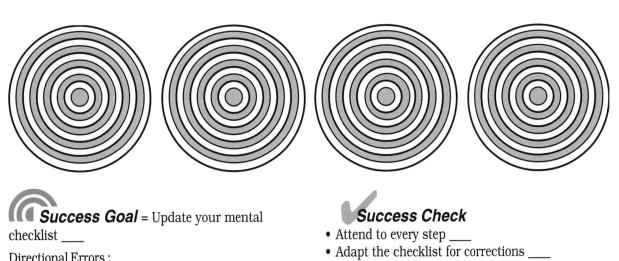

**Success Goal** = Update your mental checklist ____

Directional Errors :_____

Possible Causes: _____

_____

_____

Items Added to Checklist:_____

_____

_____

**Success Check**
• Attend to every step ____
• Adapt the checklist for corrections ____

## 7. Concentration Exercise

You can practice your concentration outside archery practices with a concentration grid. A concentration grid is a 10-by-10 grid filled with scrambled two-digit numbers starting with 00. Starting with 11, find the next number in order and put a slash (/) through it. See how many numbers you can put a slash through in one minute.

**Success Goal** = At least 25 numbers slashed in 1 minute ____

**Success Check**
• Focus on grid ____
• Push other thoughts away ____

**To Increase Difficulty**
• Extend the time to 90 seconds and the numbers slashed to 40.

| 85 | 61 | 55 | 84 | 27 | 51 | 78 | 59 | 52 | 13 |
|----|----|----|----|----|----|----|----|----|----|
| 57 | 29 | 33 | 28 | 60 | 92 | 04 | 97 | 90 | 31 |
| 86 | 18 | 70 | 32 | 96 | 65 | 39 | 80 | 77 | 49 |
| 46 | 88 | 00 | 76 | 87 | 71 | 95 | 98 | 81 | 01 |
| 42 | 62 | 34 | 48 | 82 | 89 | 47 | 35 | 17 | 10 |
| 94 | 69 | 56 | 44 | 67 | 93 | 11 | 07 | 43 | 72 |
| 14 | 91 | 02 | 53 | 79 | 05 | 22 | 54 | 74 | 58 |
| 66 | 20 | 40 | 06 | 68 | 99 | 75 | 26 | 15 | 41 |
| 45 | 83 | 24 | 50 | 09 | 64 | 08 | 38 | 30 | 36 |
| 19 | 12 | 63 | 03 | 73 | 21 | 23 | 16 | 37 | 25 |

## *8. Verbal Cue Drill*

Shoot two ends of six arrows each from any distance you choose. Prepare your shot to the point of aiming. When you are ready to aim, say to yourself, "aim, aim, aim," until the release occurs.

*Success Goal* = 12 repetitions with focus on the bull's-eye at release ___

*To Increase Difficulty*
• Bring a friend along to watch you shoot.
• Have the friend talk while you are aiming.

✔ *Success Check*
• Proceed through checklist ___
• Refocus if mind wanders ___

## *9. Hand and Arm Relaxation*

Practice this drill in a quiet place where you can sit or lie down carefully. Go through the following steps:

a. Bend your right hand back. Hold for 10 seconds, then relax. Repeat.

b. Bend your right hand forward. Hold for 10 seconds, then relax. Repeat.

c. Repeat "a" and "b" with your left hand.

d. Repeat "a" with half as much tension on your hold. Do the same with "b."

e. Repeat "d" with your left hand.

f. Repeat "a" with just enough tension that you feel the hold. Do the same with "b."

g. Repeat "f" with your left hand.

h. Bend at your right elbow. Hold for 10 seconds, then relax. Repeat. Repeat with your left elbow.

i. Repeat "h" with half as much tension.

j. Repeat "h" with barely enough tension to feel.

k. Clench your fist and tighten your whole right arm. Hold for 10 seconds, then relax. Repeat.

l. Repeat "k" with your left arm.

*Success Goal* = Work through the preceding relaxation list to achieve a relaxed state ___

*To Increase Difficulty*
• Add the legs and feet.
• Add the trunk.

✔ *Success Check*
• Think only about one body part at a time ___

## 10. Visualization

Practice this exercise in a quiet place where you can sit or lie comfortably. You can play quiet music if you like. Close your eyes. Imagine you are lying on a warm, sunny beach. Try to imagine how the sand and sun feel. Then try to imagine the sound of the ocean. Add more and more detail to your mental picture. Or imagine being in any location that you consider relaxing.

**Success Goal** = Achieve a more relaxed state than you were in previously ___

**Success Check**
• Put your mind in the imagined environment ___

**To Decrease Difficulty**
• Play relaxation music compatible with your imagined location.

## 11. Mental Rehearsal

At a regular practice session, shoot as you normally do. But after any shot you consider a mistake, mentally rehearse the feel of a good shot and see the arrow hitting the bull's-eye before taking your next shot.

**Success Goal** = Mentally rehearse 12 shots ___

**Success Check**
• Proceed through mental checklist ___

## 12. Imagery Practice

Sit quietly with your eyes closed. Practice imaging by trying to see every detail of a close friend. Make the image as vivid as possible, almost like you were seeing this friend on television. When you can do this exercise well, picture your bow, including every detail possible. Then picture yourself performing with the bow. See every detail and hear the sounds that accompany shooting. Feel your muscles as they tense or relax. Note that you can picture your performance from the outside as if you were seeing yourself on television or from the inside as it feels to perform.

**Success Goal** = Practice imagery for 4 minutes ___

**Success Check**
• See more and more detail ___
• Stay relaxed ___

## *13. Thought Stopping*

This drill uses the following examples of negative statements about archery performance. Write a positive counterpart to these statements. Verbalize these statements. Then write several negative statements you find yourself saying and their positive counterparts. Verbalize the positive ones several times.

**Success Goal** = Write 6 positive statements about archery performance ___

| **Negative Statements** | **Your Statements** |
| --- | --- |
| "It is so windy I cannot keep the arrows on the target" | _____ |
| "I can't shoot well from 40 yards" | _____ |
| "I'm afraid I'll miss the whole target" | _____ |

Your additional negative statements:

1. _____ to
_____

2. _____ to
_____

**Success Check**

• Think positive ___

## *14. Goal Setting*

Athletes often overlook setting goals for performance on several levels. For example, you can set goals for the very near future or the distant future. Considering your recent archery performance, write goals for the following timelines listed. Also, give a target date for achieving your long-term goals.

**Success Goal** = Establish goals in 4 time frames ___

| **Your Goals** | **Target Date** |
| --- | --- |
| a. Next Practice: _____ | _____ |
| _____ | |
| b. Short-Term: _____ | _____ |
| _____ | |
| c. Intermediate: _____ | _____ |
| _____ | |
| d. Long-Term: _____ | _____ |
| _____ | |

**Success Check**

• Keep goals realistic ___

## MENTAL SKILLS SUCCESS SUMMARY

Following the mental checklist you designed in the Keys to Success figure 7.1 should improve your consistency from shot to shot. This checklist also keeps your mind focused on the task at hand and gives negative thoughts little opportunity to invade your thinking!

You can strengthen the mental skills outlined in figure 7.2 by practice. Use the drills to improve your mental skills both away from and on the shooting range. Good mental skills are no more accidental than good shooting skills. Both must be practiced. The time spent practicing good mental skills will return to you in years of archery enjoyment. Your goals and expectations will be realistic, and you will stay relaxed and feel competent when shooting.

# STEP 8

## FINE-TUNING: MAKING THE BOW WORK FOR YOU

Great archers are often described as machines. They appear to repeat the exact movements, and go though the same routine on each and every shot. They're human, however. Their movements vary slightly from shot to shot and day to day. They have good days and bad days, just like you.

In a sport such as archery, shooters are very dependent upon their equipment. Equipment determines how well arrows fly, even when you use perfect form. State-of-the-art equipment is complex and can be adjusted in many ways. Which way is best? The only answer is the equipment setup that produces the tightest arrow groups for you on both your good days and bad days. The process of selecting arrows and adjusting various settings on bows to yield the tightest arrow groups is called tuning. Probably no two archers would tune their equipment and arrive at exactly the same equipment setup.

## Why Tune Your Equipment Yourself?

Because you have slight variations in your setup and movement from shot to shot, you can expect arrows aimed at the same spot to land in an area on a target, not the exact same spot. You also will sometimes make mistakes in executing shots. Your ideal equipment setup should minimize the effects of normal variations and mistakes in shooting. You know your setup is good if it yields tight arrow groups. You can imagine that if a group of well-shot arrows were to fall in a wide area, your variations and mistakes would only cause the arrows to be more dispersed!

In part, you achieve tight arrow groups with smooth arrow flight. The "cleaner" your bow launches your arrows, the less arrows porpoise (wobble up and

down) or fishtail (wobble side to side) in flight. Smooth-flying arrows travel faster, minimizing the time during which any mistake on your part can affect the arrow. Ideally, tuning achieves good clearance for the arrow as it leaves the bow and eliminates all porpoising and fishtailing of arrows in flight (see the section of appendix B on the archer's paradox, p. 148). The combination of settings that achieve this goal is unique to you and your equipment. By tuning your equipment yourself, you can be assured that your equipment is maximizing your performance, and you can make timely adjustments to your equipment as needed.

## How to Make Initial Adjustments to Your Bow

You must make several determinations and decisions before you tune your bow. These decisions include the bow's draw weight, the bow's string height, and the bow's tiller (the perpendicular distance between the string and each limb, measured where the limb attaches to the handle riser); your draw length, the arrow shaft size, fletching type and size, and tip weight; and the stabilizer setup. Changes in any of these factors could make it necessary to retune the bow. Some of these factors are more pertinent for recurve bows than compound bows, and others more pertinent for compound bows than recurve bows.

### Recurve Bows

First, you must determine your bow's draw weight and your arrow length to choose an arrow size. Your draw length is needed to determine your arrow length. If you have not checked your draw length recently, recheck it before purchasing arrows and tuning your

### Table 8.1 Recommended Brace Heights and Ranges for Recurve Bows

| Recurve bow length (inches) | Suggested starting height (inches) | Height range (inches) |
|---|---|---|
| 64 | 8 1/4–8 1/2 | 7 3/4–9 |
| 66 | 8 3/8–8 5/8 | 8–9 1/4 |
| 68 | 8 1/2–8 3/4 | 8 1/4–9 1/2 |
| 70 | 8 5/8–8 7/8 | 8 1/2–9 3/4 |

bow to them (see step 1, drill 2, p. 31). Most bow shops have a scale that gives the draw weight of a bow at any draw length (see figure 8.1a). Bows are labeled for draw weight at a standard draw length, but you should make sure the label is correct and the appropriate adjustment is made for draw lengths longer or shorter than the standard.

The string, or brace, height of a recurve bow (the distance between the bow's pivot point and the string) must be set before tuning. The bowstring's length fixes the string height. For straight-limb bows, you should use a string length that results in a string height from six to eight inches. For recurve bows, the string height should be approximately eight inches (see table 8.1). Manufacturers typically specify a string height for their quality recurve bows. You can adjust the string height from this starting point.

The sound of the bow upon release is often a good indicator of the ideal string height for a given bow and archer; the string height that results in the quietest action is the ideal one. You can make slight changes in string height by twisting or untwisting the bowstring. Obviously, twisting the bowstring shortens its length and increases the string height. The twists should always be in the same direction as the center serving. Never remove all the twists from a bowstring. It should have six to ten twists to keep it round and without flat spots that plane in the air upon release and slow its speed. On the other hand, the increased friction of too many twists increases the likelihood of string breakage.

Select your arrow rest and install it before tuning your bow. An arrow rest used in combination with a cushion plunger is best because the plunger allows both for movement of the pressure point in and out and for independent adjustment of the spring tension. If you are using a cushion plunger, adjust the arrow rest support arm so that the center of the arrow shaft is at the center of the cushion plunger button when the shaft rests on the support arm.

Before tuning, install any accessories you plan to use, such as stabilizers, a bowsight, a draw check, and a kisser button. Changes in accessories, especially those that can affect arrow clearance or weight of the bowstring, can affect the tuning.

### Compound Bows

You must follow several steps before tuning a compound bow. Some steps are similar to those involved in setting up a recurve bow; others are unique. First, have your compound bow set for your draw length. This procedure should have been done at the pro shop when you purchased your bow. You can follow the instructions that came with the bow to change the draw length yourself, but this procedure requires unscrewing the limb bolts to take all the tension off the cables. A pro shop has a bow press that enables you to instantaneously adjust the draw length.

Next, you should adjust and tighten the cable guard if your bow is equipped with an adjustable guard. The cable guard holds the cables away from the nocked arrow so it can pass freely upon release. Set the cable guard to route the cables just out of the way, but no farther than necessary. On some compound bows, changes in cable guard position slightly affect the draw length, which is why you need to make this adjustment before tuning your bow.

Compound bows have a draw weight range. Before setting the desired draw weight, you must adjust a compound bow's tiller (see figure 8.1b). The tiller is the perpendicular distance between the string and each limb measured from where the limb attaches to the handle riser. Manufacturers often recommend the tiller settings for their bows. Most settings are such that the top limb tiller is approximately one-eighth of an inch longer than the bottom limb tiller. You can measure the tiller with a bow square or metal tape.

To change the tiller, use an Allen wrench to turn the limb bolt clockwise to lengthen the tiller or counterclockwise to shorten it. On modern, two-wheel compound bows, the exact tiller measurements are not as important as setting them and checking regularly to be sure that they remain the same.

After you set the tiller on your compound bow, you can measure the draw weight with a scale and adjust the poundage by turning the limb bolts with an Allen wrench. The draw weight should be the weight you can shoot with good form over the course of a shooting round. A clockwise turn increases the poundage. Be sure to adjust the top and bottom bolts

an equal number of turns to maintain the tiller ratio.

Manufacturers also specify the brace height of a compound bow. You can adjust this height by using the same methods used for recurve bows (see preceding section). As with a recurve bow, you should install the arrow rest and all accessories on your compound bow before tuning it. These accessories include stabilizers, a bowsight, a draw check, a kisser button, a peep sight, and any cable keepers that hold the cables in close proximity to one another.

**FIGURE 8.1** **KEYS TO SUCCESS**

# PRELIMINARY TUNING STEPS

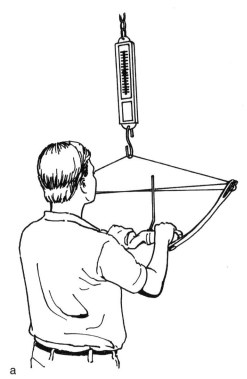

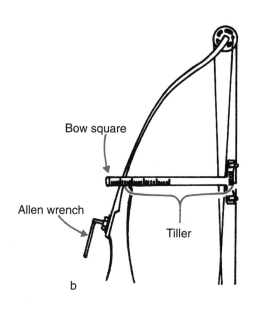

## Recurve Bows

1. Determine draw weight ___
2. Determine draw length ___
3. Set bow's string height ___
4. Position arrow rest ___
5. Install accessories ___
6. Determine arrow length ___
7. Choose arrow shaft size ___
8. Choose fletching and arrow tip ___

## Compound Bows

1. Adjust bow for draw length ___
2. Position cable guard, if necessary ___
3. Adjust bow's tiller ___
4. Adjust bow's draw weight ___
5. Position arrow rest ___
6. Install accessories ___
7. Determine arrow length ___
8. Choose arrow shaft size ___
9. Choose fletching and arrow tip ___

# How to Select Your Arrows

To achieve good shooting, you must have arrows that are uniform in spine and weight and are the proper size. The arrow manufacturer can provide a chart listing one or more shaft sizes for a given bow draw weight and arrow length. Table 8.2 is the quick reference chart for Easton aluminum shafts. Directions for using the chart are given, but you must know your bow draw weight, as discussed earlier, and your

---

**Table 8.2  Shaft Selection Chart**

*Directions for Using Chart*: 1) Recurve Bows: Find your actual draw weight in the left hand vertical column and follow this band horizontally across to your arrow length. Arrow sizes in that block are most likely your best fit. Sizes in bold type are the most widely used. 2) Compound Bows: Determine your holding and peak weights on a bow scale, available at most pro shops. Add these weights together and divide by 2 to determine your equivalent compound bow weight. Find this value in the left hand column and use the chart as described above for recurve bows. Alternatively, determine your peak weight on a scale and consult the manufacturer's literature to find your bow's percent let-off. Find the peak weight in the appropriate right hand vertical column and use the table as described above.

### EASTON ALUMINUM "QUICK REFERENCE" CHART [a]

| ACTUAL RECURVE BOW WEIGHT —OR— EQUIVALENT COMPOUND BOW WEIGHT (POUNDS & KILOGRAMS) | 61.0 CM 24" | 63.5 CM 25" | 66.0 CM 26" | 68.6 CM 27" | 71.1 CM 28" | 73.7 CM 29" | 76.2 CM 30" | 78.7 CM 31" | 81.3 CM 32" | COMPOUND PEAK BOW WEIGHT 30% LET-OFF | 50% LET-OFF |
|---|---|---|---|---|---|---|---|---|---|---|---|
| | | | | CORRECT ARROW LENGTH (INCHES & CENTIMETERS) | | | | | | (POUNDS & KILOGRAMS) | |
| 20-25# (9.1-11.3 KG.) | 1416⊙ | 1516⊙⊠ | 1516⊙⊠, 1518⊙ | 1518⊙ | 1616⊙⊠, 1614⊠, 1616⊙⊠ | 1714⊠, 1713⊙, 1714⊠ | 1813⊙ | 1913⊙ | | 24-29# (10.9-13.2 KG.) | 27-33# (12.3-15.0 KG.) |
| 25-30# (11.3-13.6 KG.) | 1516⊠ | 1516⊙⊠, 1518⊙ | 1518⊙, 1614⊠, 1616⊙⊠ | 1616⊙⊠, 1618⊙, 1713⊙, 1714⊠ | 1714⊠, 1716⊙⊠, 1814⊠ | 1716⊙⊠, 1813⊙, 1814⊠ | 1816⊙⊠, 1913⊙ | 1914⊠, 1916⊙⊠ | | 29-35# (13.2-15.9 KG.) | 33-40# (15.0-18.1 KG.) |
| 30-35# (13.6-15.9 KG.) | 1516⊙⊠, 1518⊙ | 1518⊙, 1614⊠ | 1616⊙⊠, 1618⊙, 1713⊙, 1714⊠ | 1618⊙, 1714⊠, 1716⊙⊠, 1813⊙ | 1716⊙⊠, 1813⊙, 1814⊠ | 1718⊙, 1816⊙⊠, 1913⊙ | 1818⊙, 1914⊠, 1916⊙⊠ | 1916⊙⊠, 2013⊙, 2014⊠ | 2016⊙, 2114⊙ | 35-41# (15.9-18.6 KG.) | 40-47# (18.1-21.3 KG.) |
| 35-40# (15.9-18.1 KG.) | 1518⊙, 1614⊠ | 1616⊙⊠, 1618⊙, 1713⊙ | 1618⊙, 1714⊠, 1716⊙⊠, 1813⊙ | 1716⊙⊠, 1813⊙, 1814⊠ | 1718⊙, 1816⊙⊠, 1913⊙ | 1818⊙, 1914⊠, 1916⊙⊠ | 1916⊙⊠, 2013⊙, 2014⊠ | 1918⊙, 2016⊙, 2114⊙ | 2018⊙, 2114⊙, 2115⊠, 2213⊙ | 41-47# (18.6-21.3 KG.) | 47-53# (21.3-24.0 KG.) |
| 40-45# (18.1-20.4 KG.) | 1616⊙⊠, 1618⊙, 1713⊙ | 1618⊙, 1714⊠, 1716⊙⊠, 1813⊙ | 1716⊙⊠, 1813⊙, 1814⊠ | 1718⊙, 1816⊙⊠, 1913⊙ | 1818⊙, 1914⊠, 1916⊙⊠ | 1916⊙⊠, 2013⊙, 2014⊠ | 1918⊙, 2016⊙, 2114⊙ | 2018⊙, 2114⊙, 2115⊠, 2213⊙ | 2018⊙, 2115⊠, 2213⊙ | 47-53# (21.3-24.0 KG.) | 53-60# (24.0-27.2 KG.) |
| 45-50# (20.4-22.7 KG.) | 1618⊙, 1714⊠, 1716⊙⊠, 1813⊙ | 1716⊙⊠, 1813⊙, 1814⊠ | 1718⊙, 1816⊙⊠, 1913⊙ | 1818⊙, 1914⊠, 1916⊙⊠ | 1916⊙⊠, 2013⊙, 2014⊠ | 1918⊙, 2016⊙, 2114⊙ | 2018⊙, 2114⊙, 2115⊠, 2213⊙ | 2018⊙, 2115⊠, 2213⊙ | 2117⊙, 2216⊙ | 53-59# (24.0-26.8 KG.) | 60-67# (27.2-30.4 KG.) |
| 50-55# (22.7-24.9 KG.) | | 1718⊙, 1816⊙⊠, 1913⊙ | 1818⊙, 1914⊠, 1916⊙⊠ | 1916⊙⊠, 2013⊙, 2014⊠ | 1918⊙, 2016⊙, 2114⊙ | 2018⊙, 2114⊙, 2115⊠, 2213⊙ | 2018⊙, 2115⊠, 2213⊙ | 2117⊙, 2216⊙ | 2216⊙ | 59-65# (26.8-29.5 KG.) | 67-73# (30.4-33.1 KG.) |
| 55-60# (24.9-27.2 KG.) | | | 1916⊙⊠, 2013⊙, 2014⊠ | 1918⊙, 2016⊙, 2114⊙ | 2018⊙, 2114⊙, 2115⊠, 2213⊙ | 2018⊙, 2115⊠, 2213⊙ | 2117⊙, 2216⊙ | 2216⊙ | 2219⊙ | 65-71# (29.5-32.2 KG.) | 73-80# (33.1-36.3 KG.) |

*Note*: 1413 not listed, should be used for draw lengths of less than 24" (57.6 CM) and bow weights under 20 lbs.
⊙ Indicates XX75®   ⊠ Indicates X7®
2024 Alloy (24SRT-X® , Swift®  & Game Getter® ) not listed = 1% stiffer in spine & 1% lighter in weight than XX75® .
XX75®  X7®  24SRT-X®  Swift®  Game Getter®   ® Reg. TM. Jas. D. Easton, Inc.
[a]The Easton Aluminum ''Quick Reference'' chart is from *Target archery with Easton aluminum shafts* (p. 9) by Easton Aluminum, Inc., 1981, Van Nuys, CA. Copyright 1981 by Jas. D. Easton, Inc. Reprinted by permission.

arrow length. A pro shop will have a more complete chart for Easton shafts and charts from other shaft manufacturers.

To determine your arrow length, add 1/2 to 3/4 inch to your draw length. If you're using a clicker, keep in mind that your arrow length must allow for use of the clicker. Bowhunters need extra arrow length so that when their broadheads are installed, the blades are well in front of the bow hand.

Aluminum arrow shaft sizes are designated by four digits. The first two indicate the outside shaft diameter, measured in 64ths of an inch. The second two give the aluminum tube wall thickness, measured in thousandths of an inch. For example, an 1813 shaft is 18/64 inch in diameter and 13/1000 inch in wall thickness. As you can see from table 8.2, a stiffer arrow is recommended as bow draw weight increases. A heavier arrow is recommended as arrow length increases. Keep in mind that the table gives guidelines, not definitive rules. The qualities of bow and archer may result in an arrow selection other than the recommended one. Carbon and aluminum-carbon arrows often have a different sizing system; the system for these arrows sometimes incorporates a measure of spine (stiffness). Consult a size selection chart from the manufacturer of the shaft you're considering.

With some aluminum shaft alloys, you have a choice of regular or heavyweight arrow tips. Most archers experiment to find the best tip weight. A heavier tip results in heavier arrow weight, but it is usually more effective than lighter tips in crosswind conditions. A heavier tip also makes an arrow stiffer in spine. Whenever you change tip weights, you must retune your bow. Carbon and aluminum-carbon arrows are more likely to have a point insert system, which enables you to select from a wide range of point weights and to easily change weights. The shaft manufacturer typically provides a chart of recommended starting point-plus-insert weights for these arrows.

You also must decide whether to shoot arrows fletched with feathers or plastic vanes, as well as what size fletching to use. These decisions often hinge on whether you anticipate shooting indoors or outdoors. Many archers fletch their arrows with feathers for indoor shooting and vanes for outdoor shooting to take advantage of the strengths of each type of fletching.

Feathers are lighter and can better compensate for your shooting flaws, such as a poor release. Slight contact between feathers and the arrow rest or bow window does not usually affect arrow flight as significantly as the same contact by plastic vanes. On the other hand, feathers are affected by rain and wind. Vanes are thinner and smoother than feathers and do not slow down an arrow as rapidly as feathers do. Being uniformly produced, they typically yield better arrow groupings at longer distances.

Archers using mechanical release aids typically use vanes for indoor and outdoor shooting. Because the arrow does not bend very much with mechanical release of the string, the forgiveness of feathers can be sacrificed for the consistency of vanes. Also, small vanes are sufficient to stabilize the arrow in release shooting, and it is easier to obtain good arrow clearance with small vanes.

Archers generally use the smallest size fletching that can stabilize their arrows quickly. Because large fletching increases the arrow weight, archers do not want to use unnecessarily large fletching. Many archers like to mount their fletching on the arrow shaft at a small angle, rather than aligning it precisely along the shaft's center line. The oncoming wind causes the arrow in flight to spin around its long axis, providing stability. This spinning also slows down the arrow; the greater the spin is, the slower the arrow flies. If you decide to angle the fletching and you are shooting feathers, be sure to offset the feathers so that the oncoming air contacts the rough side of the feather. Others mount their fletching straight on the shaft, preferring speed over the spinning effect.

You can experiment to determine the best combination for you, but be sure to tune your bow for the setup you decide upon and shoot arrows all fletched the same way. Changing the length or tip weight of your arrow changes the points, or nodes, around which the arrow bends as it oscillates on its flight to the target. Such a change usually means you need to retune your equipment.

## Preliminary Alignment

The tuning process is divided into two phases: preliminary alignment and fine-tuning. In the preliminary alignment, you adjust the horizontal and vertical orientations of the nocked arrow for proper arrow alignment. In the fine-tuning process, you make fine corrections for alignment and adjust the cushion plunger tension.

Your first step in preliminary alignment is to horizontally align the nocked arrow as it sits in the bow. When an arrow bends, it oscillates around two points or nodes. Ideally, the two nodes are aligned to the target when the arrow starts forward upon release. This preliminary adjustment estimates the best horizontal position for the arrow.

The most desirable starting position for your arrow depends on the type of equipment and release you are using. If you have a cushion plunger on your bow, you can screw it in or out such that the plunger button protrudes through the bow a greater or lesser amount. For a finger release, adjust the cushion plunger so that the center of a nocked arrow shaft is 1/8 inch outside the bowstring for a compound bow or 1/8 to 3/16 inch outside for a recurve bow (see figures 8.2a and 8.2b). When making this adjustment, be sure you view the arrow when the bowstring is centered to the bow. On a recurve bow, the bowstring is aligned with the center of the bow limbs. But on a compound bow, the bowstring is offset to the outside because of the eccentric pulleys. Be sure you take this fact into account when aligning the cushion plunger. When you release the bowstring, the arrow pushes against the cushion plunger, which

gives in, so that the arrow's nodes are aligned to the target as the arrow starts forward.

If you use a mechanical release, adjust the cushion plunger so the arrow is pointed straight toward the target. This orientation is also best if you are using a shoot-through rest without a cushion plunger. With a mechanical release, the arrow bends vertically, not horizontally, upon release, so you want the arrow's nodes aligned as the arrow sits in the bow. Remember, these alignments are starting points. You will make further adjustments in the fine-tuning process.

The next phase in preliminary alignment is to position the nock locator on the bowstring so that the arrow nock is approximately 1/2 inch above the line forming a perfect 90-degree angle with the string (see figure 8.2c) for a finger release and 1/4 inch above the line for a mechanical release. Ideally, you should use a clamp-on nock locator. It should be clamped on firmly but not tightly at this time. In fine-tuning, you can thread the locator up or down to make a fine adjustment, and then tightly clamp it down. If you're using Kevlar bowstrings, be careful not to clamp down the nock locator too tightly because the bowstring's strands could easily be cut.

FIGURE 8.2 | **KEYS TO SUCCESS**

# PRELIMINARY ALIGNMENT

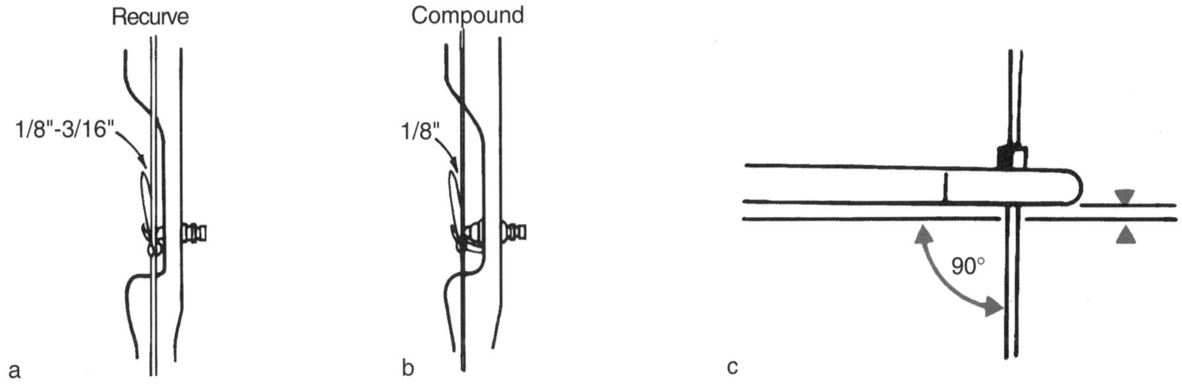

## Horizontal

1. Arrow 1/8 inch outside bowstring, compound bow ___
2. Arrow 1/8 to 3/16 inch outside bowstring, recurve bow ___
3. Arrow directly aligned, mechanical release ___

## Vertical

1. Arrow 1/2 inch above 90-degree line, finger release ___
2. Arrow 1/4 inch above 90-degree line, mechanical release ___

# Fine-Tuning

There are several methods for fine-tuning. Every archer tends to prefer one over the others. Experiment in order to find the one you prefer. The methods included here are the bare shaft and paper tuning methods. These methods are described for right-handed shooters; if you're left-handed, remember to transpose the pertinent left/right directions.

## *Bare Shaft Method*

For bare shaft tuning, you need three fletched arrows and two or three identical arrows without fletching. The first step in tuning is to check for porpoising of the arrow in flight, which means the nock end of the arrow appears to move up and down in flight (see figure 8.3).

Shoot three fletched arrows at a target from 10 to 15 yards. Then shoot two or three unfletched, but identically aimed, arrows. If the unfletched shafts hit higher on the target than the fletched shafts, move the nock locator up on the bowstring (see figure 8.5a). If the unfletched shafts hit lower than the fletched shafts, move the nock locator down. After an adjustment, repeat this process until the fletched and unfletched shafts hit at the same height on the target. Porpoising must be corrected before moving to the next step.

The second phase in bare shaft tuning is a check for fishtailing, which means the nock end of the arrow appears to move from side to side in flight (see figure 8.4). Repeat the procedure described in the preceding paragraph. If the unfletched shafts land to the left of the fletched shafts, your arrow reaction is too stiff (see figure 8.5b). If your unfletched shafts land to the right of the fletched shafts, your arrow reaction is too weak. Consult the Fine-Tuning Success Stoppers (p. 114) for corrections.

After each adjustment, repeat this process until you can bring the unfletched shafts within at least

**Figure 8.3** An arrow porpoising in flight.

**Figure 8.4** An arrow fishtailing in flight.

four inches of the fletched shafts at a distance of 15 yards. If you cannot make further adjustments to bring the unfletched shafts within four inches, you may have to change your arrow shaft size to achieve good arrow flight.

The final check in bare shaft tuning is a check for proper clearance of the arrow through the arrow rest and bow window (see figure 8.5c). This step is very important if you are using lightweight arrows, such as carbon shafts. Sprinkle talcum powder on the arrow rest and bow window. Or you can spray both the fletched end of the arrow and the arrow rest assembly with dry spray deodorant. Shoot an arrow and examine the bow. You will be able to identify places where the arrow fletching strikes the arrow rest or bow window. Arrows that strike the arrow rest or bow usually move side to side in flight, similar to fishtailing but with quicker, smaller movements. This action is often called minnowing. Consult the Fine-Tuning Success Stoppers (p. 115) for ways to correct minnowing.

Some archers use only one bare shaft when they tune. If you attempt to do so, be sure you base your adjustments on bare shaft shots that are well aimed

---

**FIGURE 8.5** | KEYS TO SUCCESS

# BARE SHAFT TUNING

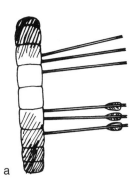

a

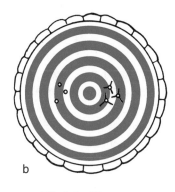

b

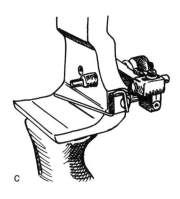

c

### Porpoising

1. Shoot three fletched arrows ___
2. Shoot three bare arrow shafts ___
3. If bare shafts strike high, move nock locator up ___
4. If bare shafts plane up, move nock locator up ___
5. If bare shafts strike low, move nock locator down ___
6. If bare shafts plane down, move nock locator down ___
7. When bare shafts are within four inches of fletched shafts, proceed to next stage ___

### Fishtailing

1. Shoot three fletched arrows ___
2. Shoot three bare shafts ___
3. If bare shafts land left, arrow reaction is too stiff ___
4. If bare shafts land right, arrow reaction is too weak ___
5. If bare shafts are within four inches of fletched shafts, proceed to next stage ___

### Clearance

1. Sprinkle arrow rest and bow window with talcum powder ___
2. Shoot arrow ___
3. Inspect bow for contact ___
4. Inspect arrow for contact ___
5. If there is contact, make corrections for minnowing ___

and well executed. You will spend considerably more time tuning your bow if you make an unnecessary or incorrect adjustment after a poorly executed shot with a bare shaft.

## The Paper Tuning Method

Paper tuning is a method of fine-tuning that has been very successful with compound bows. In order to paper tune, you need a large picture frame that can be hung two yards in front of a target at shoulder height. Tape newspaper onto the frame, then shoot arrows through the paper and use the pattern of the tear to help you make tuning adjustments.

A shooting distance of two to eight yards from the paper is used for paper tuning. You may want to start close and when the results look good, move back to make even finer adjustments. Archers using their fingers to hold and release typically stay within five yards. Archers using release aids might want to back up as far as eight yards. The tears are the largest at approximately eight yards.

Before paper tuning, check for proper clearance of the fletching as it passes the arrow rest and handle riser. As described in the previous section, sprinkle talcum powder or spray dry deodorant on the arrow fletching, the arrow rest, and handle riser (see figure 8.6a). Shoot an arrow, and then look for evidence that the fletching contacted the arrow rest or handle riser. Slight contact can sometimes be corrected by rotating the arrow nock. Severe contact can result from a nock that fits too tightly on the string or from an arrow that is too stiff. Torquing the bowstring with the draw fingers can also cause this problem. Experiment with nock size and your hand position. If these changes do not correct the problem, you may need to change arrow sizes.

As with the bare shaft tuning method, the first adjustment is for porpoising. Shoot several fletched arrows through the paper. The ideal tear pattern is a perfect hole or a hole that shows the arrow went through slightly nock high or slightly nock high and left for a right-hander (see figure 8.6b). If the hole indicates the arrow went through the paper with the nock 3/4 inch or more high, move the nock locator down. If the arrow goes through the paper nock down, move the nock locator up. It is perfectly acceptable for the arrow to be slightly nock high (as much as 1/2 inch) at this point in arrow flight because this means the arrow is probably not hitting the rest as it passes the handle riser. A tear up to one inch high may be acceptable for carbon or carbon-aluminum arrows. If you cannot correct a higher tear by moving your nocking point, you might still have clearance problems. If you use a mechanical release, your arrow shaft could be too weak so you could try a stiffer shaft, a more flexible or lighter tension shoot-through arrow rest, or a lower peak draw weight on your bow.

The next adjustment is for fishtailing. If a right-handed archer shoots arrows tearing holes with the nock left (see figure 8.6c), the arrow reaction is too weak. If a right-handed archer shoots arrows tearing nock right, the arrow reaction is too stiff. Consult the Fine-Tuning Success Stoppers (p. 114) for corrections.

As with the other methods of tuning, make adjustments in small increments and shoot several arrows through the paper afterward to check the effect of your adjustment. The ideal pattern is a perfect hole or a hole slightly nock high and left for a right-handed shooter, nock high and right for a left-handed shooter. If you shoot a compound bow and cannot correct high or low tears with tuning, have a pro shop check the timing of the roll over of your bow's eccentric wheels or cams.

FIGURE
8.6 **KEYS TO SUCCESS**

# PAPER TUNING

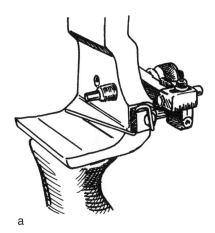

a

b

c

### Clearance

1. Sprinkle rest and window with powder ___
2. Shoot arrow, inspect for contact ___
3. Make corrections to eliminate contact and recheck ___

### Porpoising

1. Shoot several fletched arrows through paper ___
2. Examine for ideal tear pattern ___
3. If nock high or low, move nock locator ___
4. Recheck; if you can't correct it, recheck clearance ___

### Fishtailing

1. Shoot several fletched arrows through paper ___
2. If nock left, correct for weak arrow reaction ___
3. If nock right, correct for stiff arrow reaction ___

## The Final Phase of Tuning

The ultimate test to check your tuning is to shoot arrows to see that they group well. Occasionally, archers find that the tuning setup that produces the best groups is not the one that produces the most smoothly flying arrow and vice versa. Shoot ends of 8 to 10 arrows from the longest distance you plan to shoot in competition. If your arrows do not group, you might want to make further, but very fine, adjustments.

If your groups spread vertically, you can make a 1/32 inch adjustment in your nocking point. If an adjustment increases the size of your groups, return to the starting point and move in the other direction. If your groups improve and then open up with further adjustment, you probably went too far. Go back to your best setting.

If your groups spread horizontally and you shoot a compound bow, make 1/32 inch in/out adjustments of your cushion plunger. Compound bow, fingers shooters can then make 1/8 turn adjustments in cushion plunger tension. Recurve bow shooters should only make 1/8 turn adjustments in the cushion plunger. Move up 20 yards and make your left/right impact adjustments again, continuing to a shooting distance of 20 yards.

A kisser button or peep sight may need minor adjustments in its position after tuning. The need for these adjustments is a result of changes in the position of the nocking point in the fine-tuning process and the resulting changes in the position of your hand or release aid on the string.

As you can see, tuning requires time and patience.

You must be willing to experiment and to see what effect an adjustment has on arrow flight. Try to make just one adjustment at a time, shooting after each change. This process obviously requires time, but you will be rewarded in the end by knowing that your equipment is contributing the utmost to your scoring accuracy.

## FINE-TUNING SUCCESS STOPPERS

Arrows that porpoise, fishtail, or minnow in flight will compound your technique errors rather than forgive them. You should correct arrow clearance problems and arrow reaction that is too stiff or too weak. There are a variety of corrections for these problems. Try the simpler ones first.

| Error | Correction |
|---|---|
| 1. Arrow reaction is too stiff. | 1. • Decrease the spring tension on the cushion plunger.<br>• Use a weaker spring rest.<br>• Increase the draw weight of your bow if it is adjustable (one pound at a time).<br>• Use a heavier arrow point.<br>• Use a lighter bowstring.<br>• Use a weaker arrow shaft.<br>• Compound bows: Move cushion plunger in.<br>• Release shooters: Move arrow rest left; check for arrow clearance of cable and cable guard. |
| 2. Arrow reaction is too weak. | 2. • Increase the spring tension of your cushion plunger.<br>• Use a stiffer (heavier) spring rest.<br>• Decrease your bow's draw weight, if adjustable.<br>• Use a lighter arrow point.<br>• Move the pressure point out (if you do not have a cushion plunger).<br>• Compound bows: Move cushion plunger or pressure point out.<br>• Use a stiffer arrow shaft.<br>• Release shooters: Move arrow rest right. |

| Error | Correction |
|---|---|
| 3. Arrow contacts rest/bow window and minnows in flight. | 3. • Rotate the arrow nock very slightly.<br>• Trim the arrow rest support arm so that it does not protrude beyond the arrow shaft.<br>• Use a lower profile fletching.<br>• Move the cushion plunger or pressure point farther out and retune your bow for fishtailing.<br>• Make sure bowstring is not catching on something, such as a shirt pocket or sleeve. |
| 4. Arrow minnows even after corrections in #3. | 4. • Change your arrow shaft size.<br>• Change the weight of your bowstring (decrease strands if arrow reaction is stiff).<br>• Change your bowstring's center serving (a heavier serving causes stiffer arrow reaction).<br>• Change your arrows' point weight (include the insert if you use one), trying a heavier point plus insert weight if your arrow reaction is too stiff.<br>• Adjust your bow's brace height. |

FINE-TUNING

# DRILLS

## 1. Preliminary Adjustment

Your bow must be prepared for tuning, just as for shooting. Consider the bow you are now using and indicate the preliminary steps you would take before tuning it.

First, list the settings you would need to check:

1. _____

2. _____

List the adjustments you would need to make:

1. _____

2. _____

List the accessories you would install before tuning:

1. _____

2. _____

**Success Goal** = Correctly identify the preliminary steps required prior to tuning ___

**Success Check**
- Bow is set up as it will be for tuning ___
- Adjustments are within specifications ___

## 2. Arrow Setup

For each of the situations below, choose the type of arrow shaft, arrow tip, and fletching you would use. Remember that there might not be just one correct answer. Some choices can reflect your personal preferences.

1. You plan to shoot outdoor target tournaments at long distances.

Shaft type _____    Tip _____    Fletching _____

2. You plan to bowhunt.

Shaft type _____    Tip _____    Fletching _____

3. You plan to shoot indoor target tournaments.

Shaft type _____    Tip _____    Fletching _____

**Success Goal** = Choose a workable arrow setup for each situation ___

**Success Check**
- Plastic fletching is durable ___
- Carbon arrows minimize the effects of wind ___
- Field tips are closer in weight to broadheads than target tips ___

## 3. Clearance Test

Sprinkle talcum powder on the fletched end of one of your arrows, your arrow rest, and your bow window. Shoot the arrow into a target at close range. Check for contact of the fletching and the rest or bow window.

**Success Goal** = Correctly identify any arrow contact and make an appropriate adjustment ___

**Success Check**
- Wear tight-fitting clothes ___
- Trim arrow rest support arm ___

Describe what you find below:

_____

_____

Describe an adjustment you would make based on your findings if this were your own equipment:

_____

_____

## 4. Porpoising Test

Use one of the tuning methods described in this step to test for porpoising. Sketch either the paper tear if you paper tuned or the impact pattern if you used the bare shaft method.

**Success Goal** = Record the results of your porpoising test accurately and decide on an adjustment ___

Describe what if any adjustment you would make, based on your findings, of the nock locator position:

_____

_____

**Success Check**
• Rely on well-executed shots for your results ___
• Repeat poorly executed shots ___

## 5. Fishtailing Test

Assume that you have corrected for porpoising. Use one of the tuning methods to test for fishtailing. Sketch either the tear pattern if you paper tuned or the impact pattern if you used the bare shaft method.

**Success Goal** = Record the results of your fishtailing test accurately and decide on an adjustment ___

Describe an adjustment you would make, based on your findings:

_____

_____

**Success Check**
• Rely on well-executed shots for your results ___
• Repeat poorly executed shots ___

## FINE-TUNING SUCCESS SUMMARY

In archery, your success depends on your equipment as well as your form. Among tournament-level archers whose skill and practice levels are similar, the archer whose equipment performs the best will outshoot the others. Resolve to learn the most you can about your equipment and how to tune it.

Prepare your equipment by making the preliminary adjustments in figure 8.1 and the preliminary alignments in figure 8.2. Then choose a method of fine-tuning, either the bare shaft method outlined in figure 8.5 or the paper tuning method outlined in figure 8.6. When your final tuning check shows that your arrows are grouping tightly, you can be confident that your equipment is functioning at its maximum performance level.

# STEP 9

# BOWHUNTING: ADAPTING TO CONDITIONS

I t's early morning in the woods. The sun is coming up. The fall air is cool. Birds are beginning to sing. A lone bowhunter waits in a tree stand. A doe comes over the rise. The hunter's heart begin to pound. "Set bow hand," the bowhunter thinks, "Set fingers." The doe turns away, down the far path. "No problem. There's always next week."

The archers who bowhunt enjoy it for many different reasons. Probably all of them like the challenge of hunting, but some also like being in and around nature. They enjoy the peacefulness of the forest, perhaps because it is a contrast to their daily lives. Some appreciate the opportunity to observe wildlife. They look forward to hunting days all year long.

## Why Bowhunt?

Humans have bowhunted for centuries, first out of necessity, but now for the challenge of hunting and participation in a natural cycle of checks and balances on the world's animal population. Bowhunters enjoy preparing for bowhunting, testing their distance judging skills, and executing one perfect shot when the right moment comes. Many have their game meat processed and feel part of an age-old tradition. They help control the size of game herds, many of whom have lost their natural predators and would otherwise suffer the disease and starvation that accompanies overpopulation. Bowhunters also enjoy being in the woods, away from the fast pace and pressure of daily life.

Bowhunting is far from a one-weekend-a-year hobby. Bowhunters must spend countless hours preparing their equipment and practicing for that one, all-important shot. Fortunately, there are several enjoyable ways to practice for bowhunting. Some archers make bowhunting a year-round activity by participating in indoor tournaments for archers with bowhunting equipment, in field archery events, and 3-D target shoots.

## How to Bowhunt

The basic archery shot remains the same whether you are shooting at a paper target or live game. When you execute the fundamentals of a shot well, you are more likely to experience success. Bowhunting, though, requires some adaptations to the conditions under which you hunt. They are not as predictable as in target archery, and you usually get only one chance to hit your mark!

First, your stance must adapt to the terrain. Your feet might have to be farther apart or closer than ideal. You might have to straddle a fallen tree. One foot might be higher than another. You might have to crouch or kneel to get a clear shot under a branch. If you hunt from a tree stand, you might even be sitting rather than standing (see figure 9.1). As out-

**Figure 9.1** Adapting to the terrain is sometimes a challenge in bowhunting.

lined in the Bowhunting Keys to Success, figure 9.2a, start your shot by establishing a stable body position. Turn or bend at the waist as necessary to align your shoulders to your target.

You will usually wait for game with your arrow nocked. Any time you must change locations, though, place your arrow with its broadhead in a hood quiver. Injuries from falling on a broadhead can be life threatening! As your game comes into view, begin to estimate its distance from you. You will only want to take a shot if the distance is one with which you are comfortable and confident. When the game stops, estimate the distance. Later, this step discusses how to adjust this estimate for the conditions and take into account the game's angle of orientation.

As with target shooting, set your bow hand and your draw hand or mechanical release, and then draw and anchor (see figure 9.2b). Leveling your bow is particularly important because slopes, hills, and shadows can cause you to unknowingly cant your bow. Locate your aiming spot and concentrate on it. Difficult as it may be, relax your hands as you aim. After releasing the bowstring, keep your arm up (see figure 9.2c). Following through is as important in hunting as in target shooting. When hunting large game, wait 30 minutes to an hour before trailing your game. If a wounded animal senses it is being pursued, it may run, covering a long distance and making it more difficult for you to track.

| FIGURE 9.2 | KEYS TO SUCCESS |
| --- | --- |

# BOWHUNTING

a

b

c

### Stance

1. Stabilize body position ___
2. Nock arrow ___
3. As game moves within range, determine if shot is possible ___
4. Wait for game to stop ___
5. Estimate distance ___
6. Adjust distance estimate for conditions ___
7. Decide if angle of game affords a good shot ___

### Draw and Aim

1. Set bow hand ___
2. Set draw hand or mechanical release ___
3. Draw and anchor ___
4. Align string and shaft and level bow ___
5. Locate aiming spot and concentrate on target ___

### Release and Follow-Through

1. Maintain back tension ___
2. Keep hands relaxed ___
3. Relax draw hand or trigger release ___
4. Keep bow arm up ___
5. Wait 30 minutes to one hour to trail game ___

## *Distance Judging*

The unique challenge of bowhunting compared to target shooting is judging your distance from your target. To be a successful hunter, you cannot rely on a lucky guess of distance. Rather, you should establish a system for judging distance and practice using it, just as you practice shooting. At least some of your practice should be in the same terrain as you hunt.

One system you can use is to spot a reference point 20 yards away. Do this by spotting five-yard increments from your location to the reference point. You can then estimate a distance to a farther or nearer target from this point. Twenty yards is a natural reference point for many archers because they commonly practice indoors at this distance. You can double-check your estimate by picking a point halfway between your location and the target and estimating your distance to this target. If doubling this distance is too different than your first estimate, repeat your judgments.

You should also get to know how many of your normal walking steps correspond to a known distance. When practicing your distance judging, take a shot at a target based on your estimate. Then walk off the distance to see how accurate your estimate was. If your shot is off the mark, you will know whether your error was in estimating your distance from the target or in executing your shot.

Shadows in wooded areas sometimes make it difficult for you to judge distance accurately. Some hunters report that they overestimate a distance in the shadows. Practice in shadows to find out what your tendencies are. Shadows also make it difficult to maintain your aim on game because the natural coloring of game animals is to provide a camouflage effect. Hunters commonly report that their aim tends to drift low or drift toward a patch of sunlight on the animal's back. Practice with paper animals or 3-D targets in shadowy conditions to learn your tendencies and overcome or compensate for them.

Some hunters use a range finder, a device that measures the distance to a location for you. Others enjoy the challenge of estimating distances and consider this challenge a fundamental part of the hunting experience. Range finders are usually prohibited in competitive tournaments for archers practicing their hunting skills.

## *Shooting on Hills*

Shooting on hills affects your shot alignment and your shooting distance. When you shoot up and down hills, especially steep ones, your bow must be pointed acutely up or down. Learn to bend from the waist to shoot so that you can maintain the best alignment of your upper body, keeping your shoulders level and your arms in line (see figure 9.3).

**Figure 9.3** Bend from the waist when shooting on hills.

The sight setting you use for an up or down hill shot of approximately 15 degrees or more, up or down, is slightly off the linear distance from you to your target. You will need to use a sight setting for a shorter distance. How much you should adjust depends in part on your arrow velocity, the weight of your arrow, and the angle to the target. Because gravity acts to slow an uphill shot or speed up a downhill shot, the arrow does not travel the near-perfect parabolic trajectory it does with a horizontal shot (see figure 9.4).

How much should you adjust for hills? If you shoot light poundage, or are taking a long shot, you will

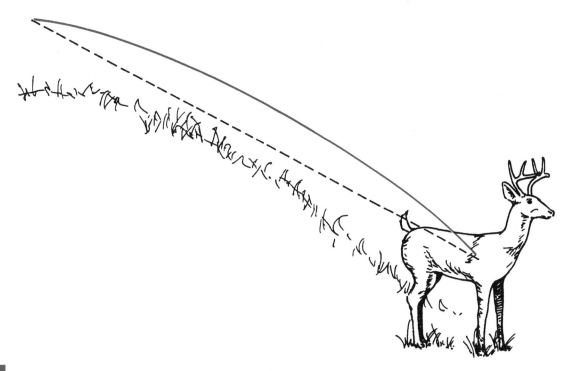

**Figure 9.4** An arrow does not travel at a near-perfect parabolic trajectory on hills.

need a larger adjustment. Long downhill shots, in particular, call for an adjustment in your sight setting. In order to learn how much to compensate for this effect on uphill and downhill shots, you must practice these shots regularly. Remember that if you later make an equipment adjustment that affects your arrow speed, you should test the effect of this change on your sight setting adjustment.

Sometimes you will have shots across the side of a hill. Side hills do not change your distance to the target, but create an illusion that causes many shooters to let their bow drift down the hill during aiming and follow-through. To avoid this drift, aim on the uphill side of your ideal hit zone or use a bowsight with a level (the rules of competitive tournaments for those with bowhunting equipment often preclude use of a level in competition).

## Where to Aim

The goal in hunting is to always kill rather than wound game animals so that the game can be retrieved and the animal dies as quickly as possible. Know the anatomy of the game you are hunting, especially the location of the heart and lungs. The most effective kill shots are those through the heart and lungs, although shots through major arteries, the liver, stomach, or kidneys can cause severe bleeding and result in a successful kill. You should also know the location of major bones in order to avoid shots that would strike bone rather than the chest cavity or vital organs.

One way for you to learn the locations of the vital organs of the game you want to hunt is to practice with paper animal targets, silhouettes, or 3-D targets that have these organs marked. Practicing with 3-D targets also helps you to learn which positions of the animal afford a good shot (see figure 9.5). If

**Figure 9.5** 3-D targets help show proper positions for a good shot.

you cannot aim a successful shot to the vital organs without hitting a major bone, you are better off passing up the shot until the animal changes positions or waiting for another opportunity altogether. Working with 3-D targets will also make you realize that when the game is angled rather than broadside to you, the "kill zone" shrinks in size (see figure 9.6).

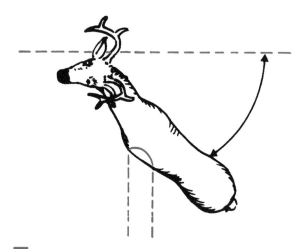

**Figure 9.6** The "kill zone" shrinks in size when the game is angled.

## Practicing for Hunting

Although hunting involves few shots, you must be well-practiced to assure yourself of success. You can practice for hunting in a variety of ways. First, indoor practice at a short distance is an excellent way to practice shot execution. You can more easily judge whether your shot execution is good when you are indoors rather than outdoors where there are more variables to influence your performance. You know that your scores reflect your shooting and not the elements or a poor estimate of distance. Conditions are better controlled, too, for trying new equipment and tuning equipment.

For a change of pace indoors, hunters can use paper animal targets for practice. Some indoor ranges sponsor bowhunting leagues where shooters take shots that simulate hunting. For example, some shots may be from a sitting or kneeling position and shooting distances may vary from shot to shot or end to end.

Outdoor target practice can also contribute to your bowhunting skills. You can practice at longer dis-

tances and obtain good sight settings. You can practice using your bowsight at odd distances, such as 23 yards or 37 yards. Most bowhunters practice at a maximum distance of 50 yards. At longer distances, even a small error in judging distance can result in your arrow being far off its mark. The risk of wounding rather than killing your game is not worth taking a shot over 50 yards.

Field archery is an excellent and fun way to practice for bowhunting. Field ranges are typically 14 targets set out in golf-course fashion, usually in a wooded area. Each target is a different distance and set on different terrain. Distances are marked. You can practice uphill and downhill shots, shots in the shadows and the sun, and shots with level and unlevel footing. You can shoot field archery with the exact equipment setup you would use for hunting, except with field tips in your arrows rather than broadheads.

3-D rounds are the type of competitive shooting closest to actual hunting. 3-D refers to the targets, usually foam animals of varying size placed in natural settings in the woods. You are given a location from which to shoot, but the distance is unmarked. Most 3-D competitions are shot with field tips, too, but occasionally broadhead rounds are held. 3-D targets are helpful in learning where to aim at various game animals standing at various angles. They also help you practice maintaining your aim at a location on the dark coat of a game animal, something quite different than aiming at a gold bull's-eye!

If you will be hunting from a tree stand, practice shooting at targets you place around the tree stand. This practice particularly helps with distance judgments. If you must practice away from the woods, consider using an elevated platform.

Although repetitive practice is beneficial for hunting, you should also practice taking single shots at different distances. This type of practice disciplines you to put together one critical shot perfectly, the first time. You otherwise may find yourself getting lazy with multiple practice shots from the same location.

Because your footing may be unlevel or awkwardly positioned in hunting, or you may be seated in a tree stand, simulate these conditions in your practice. You must learn to draw with good upper body alignment, even if you cannot position your lower body as you prefer.

# Equipment Adaptations

Bowhunting equipment has changed greatly with the advent of the compound bow. The compound has become the bow of choice for hunters, although some archers enjoy "traditional" hunting days on which hunters are restricted to long bows. As a rule, the compound bow allows you to shoot at a higher poundage, resulting in a faster arrow with less arc. The compound bow makes it easier for smaller archers, youths, and individuals with disabilities to hunt. It is also shorter and easier to carry through the woods or shoot from a tree stand.

A typical bowhunting setup consists of a compound bow, often with cam-shaped eccentric wheels and an overdraw, a short stabilizer, and a hunting bowsight (see figure 9.7). Cam-shaped eccentric wheels provide you with more arrow speed than round eccentrics. Cam bows are not as smooth in their draw as

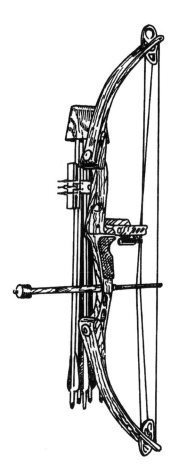

**Figure 9.7** A cam bow.

other compound bows. Because hunters shoot fewer arrows than target archers, however, many trade smoothness for speed.

The overdraw, which moves the arrow rest closer to the archer than the bow handle, makes it possible for you to use a shorter, lighter, and therefore faster arrow. Small bow hand errors upon release of the shot, though, are magnified when you use an overdraw. Again, many hunters trade precision accuracy for speed when using the overdraw. The hunting stabilizer is shorter than that on a typical target bow. This arrangement provides some of the benefits of a stabilizer without making the equipment setup too cumbersome to carry in the woods.

Hunting sights are not extended very far from the bow for the same reason. As discussed earlier, hunting sights typically have four or five pin apertures that you can set for various, usually even, distances. A common setup would be for 10, 20, 30, 40, and 50 yards. When you have an odd-distance shot, such as 25 yards, you align the bowsight so that 20 and 30 yards pins are approximately equidistant around the kill zone; or if you estimate your shooting distance to be 22 yards, you could aim your 20 yard pin slightly above the kill zone. You can see why it is advantageous to hunt with higher poundage, faster arrows, and therefore a lower trajectory. In fact, some archers with high poundage bows and fast arrow speed need only one or two pins on their bowsights.

Most bowhunters use a quiver mounted on the side of the bow. Your arrows are then handy, but the setup is still compact. The hunting quiver has a hood to shield the broadheads mounted on the arrows. Broadheads come in a variety of styles, with two to six blades (see figure 9.8a). Some are better suited to certain game, but there is a large degree of personal preference in the choice of broadheads. One thing all broadheads have in common is their sharpness. They must be handled with extreme care in order not to cut either the archer or the bowstring! Never climb or walk the woods with an arrow and broadhead in hand because you might fall on the broadhead.

Bowhunters usually practice with field points installed on their arrows (see figure 9.8b) These points are closer in weight to broadheads than are target points. They can be easily replaced by a broadhead when hunting because both points screw into the same insert. You still must sight in your broadheads

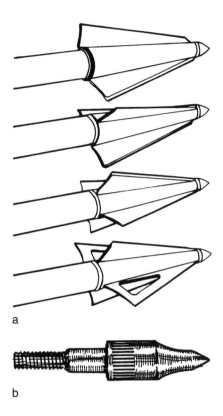

**Figure 9.8** (a) Broadhead arrows used for hunting. (b) A screw-in field point.

when installing them. It is important to align the shaft of the broadhead with the arrow shaft. If it is crooked, the arrow may "plane" on its flight to the target. A large piece of Styrofoam is good for sighting in because broadheads ruin target butts quickly and are banned on most ranges. Most hunters find that large fletching better stabilizes their arrows, given the heavy broadhead. They also prefer plastic vanes over feath-

ers because of the range of weather conditions encountered when hunting.

Bowhunters use a blunt rubber or metal tip when hunting small game, such as rabbit or squirrel. These tips kill by impact force, usually instantaneously. A broadhead would destroy too much edible meat.

Some bowhunters like to shoot with their fingers, and others prefer a release aid. When deciding which you will use, consider how quickly you can get your shot set up. Hunting does not provide the luxury of time that target shooting does. If it takes too long to set a mechanical release, you might miss your opportunity. Some hunters use releases that are quickly set. These release aids would probably not be the best for precision target shooting, but they are acceptable for hunting.

Hunters make other adaptations in their equipment setup because hunting equipment must be more durable and stand up to extremes in temperature and moisture. You may consider using a heavier, but less flexible arrow rest than target archers or using a shooting glove rather than a finger tab. Most hunting equipment comes in a dark color or a camouflage pattern. Some bowhunters like to paint their own camouflage patterns on their equipment.

Compared to target archery equipment, bowhunting equipment is compact. Bowhunters trade some precision in shooting for arrow speed and equipment durability. The basic hunting shot, though, has much in common with the basic target shot. Those archers who can execute good shots repetitiously with good T-form are likely to be successful in hunting, and those who merely hope everything will fall in place when the time comes are likely to be disappointed.

## BOWHUNTING SUCCESS STOPPERS

Many errors in bowhunting come from rushing the shot. Make sure that you take your time, estimate and double-check your distance, adjust for up or down angles, level your bow, and steady your aim before releasing the bowstring. Remember that other opportunities will come if the conditions are not right for a good shot.

| Error | Correction |
|---|---|
| 1. Arrow sails over back of target. | 1. Adjust your distance estimate to a shorter shot if shooting more than 15 degrees up or down hill, or down a from a tree stand. |
| 2. Arrow tails off toward downhill on a side-of-hill shot. | 2. Maintain follow-through on a side-of-hill shot. You can also aim slightly uphill in the kill area. |
| 3. You are too nervous to steady your aim. | 3. Practice visualizing your shot before a hunting trip and while waiting to spot game. |

## BOWHUNTING

# DRILLS

### 1. Indoor Practice

Indoor practice allows you to perfect your shot without dealing with some of the elements outdoors. You can also simulate hunting conditions to some extent. Obtain five animal targets of varying types and sizes. Take four shots at each target: one standing, one kneeling, one standing on a stable platform or chair, and one with an open stance. If you can, also vary your distance from the target. Score five points for each arrow in the kill zone on the target, three points for each arrow in the wound zone, one point for hitting somewhere else on the animal, and zero points for a miss. Total your score, and then repeat the round.

**Success Goal** = A higher score on the second round than the first ___

**Success Check**
- Adjust sight setting for downhill shot ___
- Square shoulders to target ___
- Maintain alignment ___

**To Increase Difficulty**
- Use smaller targets.
- Change distance for each shot.
- Change angle for each shot.

**To Decrease Difficulty**
- Use larger targets.
- Shoot all shots from a standing position.

## 2. Field Archery

Locate a field archery range in your geographic area and shoot a field archery round. Field ranges typically have 14 targets, varying in shooting distance from 20 feet to 80 yards. The shooting stakes are marked distances from the targets. If you do not have the equipment or sight settings to shoot the long distances, you can shoot these targets from a shorter distance. A sign at each target tells you what to do because field ranges do not have to be arranged with targets in any particular order. Field target faces are black and white. You can score them with five points for the bull's-eye, four for the white rings, and three for the black rings, or five, four, three, two and one for each of the rings. Total your score for the 14 targets.

**Success Goal** = Improve your score every time you shoot a field round ___

**Success Check**
- Maintain upper body alignment despite footing ___
- Adjust for hills ___
- Double-check your sight setting for the marked distance ___

**To Increase Difficulty**
- Use 5-4-3-2-1 scoring.

**To Decrease Difficulty**
- Use "youth" shooting distances.
- Use animal targets.

## 3. Animal Round

On the field range you located for drill 2, shoot an animal round. Bring a pair of binoculars with you. The shooting stakes for an animal round are at uneven distances, such as 23 or 32 yards. Paper targets of game animals are used. Each target is marked with a kill zone and wound zone, usually the outline of the animal. Shoot an initial arrow. If it lands in the kill zone, record 20 points. If it lands in the wound area, record 16 points. If your first arrow misses, shoot a second arrow. Record 14 points for a kill or 10 points for a wound. Again, if your second arrow misses, shoot a third arrow. Record 8 points for a kill and 4 for a wound. You only have to shoot a subsequent arrow if you do not score with the previous arrow. Total your score for the 14 targets.

**Success Goal** = Improve your score every time you shoot an animal round ___

✔**Success Check**
• Locate the ideal area for aiming ___
• Adjust for hills ___
• Follow through ___

## 4. 3-D Animal Round

Find out from a local bowhunting club when a 3-D round will be held and whether field tips or broadheads will be used. Go through the round on the indicated day and record your score. The center "vital" scoring area of the animal model is worth 10 points, the outer vital area is worth 8 points, and the remainder of the animal's body is worth 5 points.

**Success Goal** = Improve your score every time you shoot a 3-D round ___

✔**Success Check**
• Estimate your shooting distance in five-yard increments ___
• Double-check your distance estimate ___
• Adjust for conditions ___
• Maintain your aim until steady on the target ___

## 5. Tree Stand Practice

If you will be bowhunting from a tree stand, practice from an elevated position so that you learn to judge your distance taking into account the "downhill" angle. You can shoot from a platform if one is available, or from a ladder. Swimming pool ladders with a platform at the top are well suited for this drill. Place the ladder about 20 yards from a target butt. Use an animal target. Shoot four arrows, and then score your shots. Reposition the ladder closer to the target, and then shoot four more arrows. Repeat this drill until you have shot 20 arrows and total your score.

**Success Goal** = Improve your 20 arrow score every time ___

✔ **Success Check**
• Adjust shooting distance for downhill shot ___

**To Increase Difficulty**
• Mix up your shooting distances.
• Include distances up to 30 yards.

---

### BOWHUNTING SUCCESS SUMMARY

Most archers can hardly resist the many ways to enjoy archery. Some target archers never hunt, but enjoy field and 3-D rounds. Some who only intended to hunt eventually take up target archery. Adapting your equipment and your shot for conditions is part of the challenge of shooting archery.

In this step, you learned how to adapt your shot and your equipment for hunting, and you learned various ways of practicing for bowhunting. Ask a partner or friend to use the Keys to Success checklists in figure 9.2 to rate your success in bowhunting. If you are planning to bowhunt, you will probably want to read more about hunting techniques, including camouflaging, calling game, trailing game after a successful shot, and field dressing your kill.

# STEP
## 10
# COMPETITIVE SHOOTING: PUTTING YOUR SKILLS ON THE LINE

Probably no group was more touched than the archery participants in the 1992 Olympics when an archer lit the Olympic torch with a flaming arrow. This opening ceremony gave them a special memory in addition to a special event in their lives, representing their countries in Olympic competition. Sharing this event with the best archers in the world was probably a long-standing goal for most. Although few archers can have this experience, every archer can come together with others to shoot in tournaments and weekly leagues.

Submitting your skills to the test of a tournament provides a landmark for which you can prepare, bringing your mental and physical skills together. The results also motivate you to continue practicing and striving for new goals. This step will familiarize you with tournament shooting and give you an opportunity to shoot a tournament score, either alone or with a group of archers.

## Why Participate in Tournaments?

Throughout learning a skill such as archery, you undoubtedly find it helpful to have clear goals. This is particularly true once you have learned the basics and need continued practice and refinement to reach a higher level. Shooting for a score provides a basis for setting goals by score; you can set your sights on obtaining an appropriately higher score the next time you compete.

Monitoring your scores over time tells you how you are progressing; scoring is a source of feedback on your archery skill progress. If you improve upon your previous scores, it is likely that your form is good

and you are on the right track. A drop in score can signal that you have unknowingly fallen into a bad habit. You can then review your form for the basics and re-establish your form. Archery is the type of sport in which the competition is within more than it is against another archer. Yet scores also provide a means of comparing your skill with that of other archers.

## How to Score in a Tournament

The first step toward participating in a tournament is to learn the scoring procedures used in archery. To compare your performance with that of other archers, you must score the arrows shot consistently. Otherwise, you would obtain very different scores if, for example, one time you gave arrows cutting two rings the higher value and another time you gave them the lower value.

Scores must also be recorded the same way, particularly in a tournament with many people shooting. Questions may arise regarding the accuracy of a score at the conclusion of shooting, and the scorecard is the official and permanent record of what really happened (see figure 10.1a). Also, some tournaments break ties by counting the number of hits on the target, the number of bull's-eyes, and so on. All archers must be aware of scoring procedures and must keep score accurately in order to compare their performances.

When shooting in a tournament, each archer is assigned to a target at check-in. Scorecards are either given to the archer or placed at the assigned target. Typically four archers are assigned to a target (see figure 10.1b). These archers perform specific scoring duties, either by assignment of the tournament officials or by mutual agreement of the archers. One archer serves as target captain and calls out the value of each arrow on the target, archer by archer. If any of the other archers disagree with a call, a tournament official is called to make the final decision on that arrow (see figure 10.1c). Two of the remaining archers keep score on independent sets of scorecards. They may cross-check each archer's end score and running score on each end so that discrepancies can be quickly rectified. The fourth archer retrieves any arrows that miss the target and may assist the target captain by checking the scores announced.

| FIGURE 10.1 | KEYS TO SUCCESS |
| --- | --- |

# SCORING IN A TOURNAMENT

a

### Scorecard

1. Obtain scorecard at check-in ___
2. Obtain target assignment ___

b

### Scoring Roles

1. One archer calls arrow values ___
2. Two archers write scores independently ___
3. One archer checks scores as announced and retrieves arrows ___

### Following Scoring Rules

1. Arrows on lines get higher value ___
2. Arrows are not touched until scored ___
3. Highest value dropped if too many arrows shot ___
4. Unshot arrows are lost to score ___
5. Undecided arrows called by tournament official ___

c

The tournament officials usually provide a scorecard that is prepared specifically for the round being shot. Figure 10.2 shows an example. The value of each arrow is entered on the card in the appropriate area, as is the end score and, often, a running score. Although the two archers keeping score on each target cross-check the scores, the archer being scored is responsible for seeing that everything on the card, including addition of the score, is in proper order before the scorecard is turned in at the conclusion of the day's shooting. In some tournaments, an archer can be disqualified for scorecard errors. When the archer is satisfied that the scorecard is correct, each scorekeeper and the archer sign the card before submitting it.

Each archery governing body and tournament can have specific rules for scoring, but the guidelines below are common to most sets of rules:

1. The traditional target face in archery consists of five concentric scoring zones: gold/yellow, red, blue, black, and white, from the center outward. Each color zone is divided into two equally sized zones by a thin line. This division results in 10 scoring zones of equal width. The innermost zone has a value of 10, the next 9, and so on through the outermost zone, with a value of 1. The target face can be of various diameters, but the scoring zones must all be of equal width.

2. The lines dividing the scoring zones are considered to be entirely within the higher scoring area. Any arrow touching a dividing line even slightly is therefore assigned the higher value. An exception is a tournament or certain scoring ends designated for inside-out scoring. Touching a line in this type of end puts an arrow in the lower scoring area. Inside-out scoring is sometimes used as a tie-breaker.

3. Arrows are scored by the position of the shafts in the target face at the time arrows are scored. Arrows sometimes enter the target at an angle or vibrate on impact, tearing into an adjacent scoring ring. These tears are ignored and the arrows are scored as they are sitting in the target face.

4. You are not allowed to touch any of the arrows in the target or the target face itself until all the arrows are scored and any questionable scores are decided upon by the appropriate official.

5. Arrows that skip into the target after striking the ground receive a score of zero.

6. If an arrow passes through the target face but not the target butt, it can be pushed back through the butt and target face to determine which scoring zone it penetrated.

7. If an arrow passes completely through the target butt or bounces out of the scoring area, and is witnessed by another archer or tournament

| Name | | | | | | | |
|------|--|--|--|--|--|--|--|
| Class | | | | | | | |
| 50 Yards | | | | | Hits | Score | |
| | | | | | | | |
| | | | | | | | |
| | | | | | | | |
| | | | | | | | |
| Distance Score | | | | | | | |
| 40 Yards | | | | | | | |
| | | | | | | | |
| | | | | | | | |
| | | | | | | | |
| | | | | | | | |
| Distance Score | | | | | | | |
| 30 Yards | | | | | | | |
| | | | | | | | |
| | | | | | | | |
| | | | | | | | |
| | | | | | | | |
| Distance Score | | | | | | | |
| Total Score | | | | | | | |

**Figure 10.2** Scorecards prepared for a Columbia round.

official, it is scored as seven points, unless the procedure in the tournament is to mark the target face at the impact point of each arrow during scoring. In this case, the pass-through or bounce-out arrow is scored according to the hole made in the target face.

8. If you shoot more arrows than the number specified to comprise an end in the round being shot, only the lowest-scoring arrows in the number comprising an end are scored. For example, if an end consists of six arrows and you shoot seven, only the lowest-scoring six arrows are scored.

9. If you do not shoot all the arrows allowed in an end and do not discover this fact before the signal to score or retire from the shooting line, you lose the chance to shoot those arrows.

10. Any arrows you shoot into a target other than the particular target assigned you are not scored.

11. An arrow that embeds itself in another arrow and does not therefore reach the target face is scored as the same value as the arrow in which it is embedded.

## How to Shoot in a Tournament

Before the day of a tournament, you have several responsibilities. One is to see that all equipment is in safe condition and in condition to provide the best possible shooting efficiency. Inspect your arrows and straighten them if necessary. Prepare a back-up bowstring and gather other spare parts such as arrow nocks, arrow rests, and so on. (See figure 10.3a). Inspect the nock locator and serving. Inspect the bowsight and tighten any screws. Inspect the arrow rest and cushion plunger or spring rest. Take the time to see that the equipment is prepared to perform as expected. Furthermore, you must obtain sight settings for all the distances that will be shot in the tournament.

Prepare carefully for outdoor tournaments. In hot and humid weather, you should take the same precautions as any other athlete. Although archery competition is not as intense as other sport contests, it can last longer, sometimes all day. Bring plenty of water and a hat. Use sunscreen and consider bringing a chair and sun umbrella. You should also pre-

pare for rain. Unless there is lightning, most tournaments continue in light rain.

A tournament official controls shooting in a tournament with the whistle signals established earlier. One whistle blast typically indicates that archers on the shooting line can begin shooting. Two blasts signal that archers can cross the shooting line to score. Three or more blasts mean that shooting should cease immediately because an emergency situation exists.

Large tournaments often have multiple shooting lines (see figure 10.3b). Half the archers assigned to a target step to the line to shoot their end, and then retire from the line while the remaining archers shoot—all before any arrows are scored. In this case, another single whistle blast is used to indicate the end of shooting for one line and to call the second group to the line. Yet another single blast indicates that the second shooting line can begin shooting.

Tournament officials often establish a time limit for shooting the arrows within an end. The time limit chosen depends upon the number of arrows shot in each end, but it is also variable across tournaments. Check to see whether a time limit will be in effect and, if so, how long it will be. Usually a warning signal is given when only 30 seconds remain in the time span.

If your equipment fails while you are on the shooting line, most tournament rules provide a time period during which you can repair or replace the equipment. If this problem should happen, raise your bow while on the shooting line to signal the tournament official. You will be given an opportunity to shoot missed arrows at a later time, provided you can make the necessary repairs in the time allowed.

Archery tournaments provide an opportunity to make new friends and renew old acquaintances. Between shooting ends, you can visit with other archers or friends, or keep to yourself as you prefer. It is common courtesy, however, not to disturb archers who are on the line shooting, either directly or indirectly by talking loudly and so on. You should never talk while on the shooting line, unless it is necessary for the purposes of the tournament. You should also avoid distracting fellow archers on either side of you by moving onto or off of the shooting line while they are at full draw. Among some archers it is traditional to remain on the shooting line until the archer on either side has finished shooting all arrows so that no archer is left on the line alone to finish shooting.

The exact number of arrows shot in a scoring round, the size of the target, and the shooting distances vary from round to round. This variety often adds to the interest of target shooting. Each round provides its own challenge. Examples of the common scoring rounds are given in table 10.1. Though these are the established archery rounds, archers are always free to design their own or modify an established round, provided all participants are made aware of the rules beforehand.

In recent years, the archery governing bodies have used new tournament formats that make watching tournaments more exciting for spectators. These formats usually involve one-on-one competition between two archers (match play) for a small number of ends with the winner advancing to shoot against another archer. Sometimes this format is used after a traditional round with the scores from that round determining seeding positions for the one-on-one competition. Eventually, two archers shoot against each other for the tournament title. Such a format truly increases the excitement of shooting and watching tournament archery.

| FIGURE 10.3 | KEYS TO SUCCESS |
|---|---|

# SHOOTING IN A TOURNAMENT

a

b

## Preparation

1. Check equipment for safety and efficiency \_\_\_
2. Gather spare parts for backup \_\_\_
3. Get sight settings for needed distances \_\_\_
4. Prepare food, drink, clothing \_\_\_

## Procedures During Shooting

1. Follow signals of tournament official \_\_\_
2. Retire from line when finished shooting \_\_\_
3. Manage your time to shoot all arrows if time is limited \_\_\_
4. Raise bow if equipment fails \_\_\_
5. Be courteous to other archers \_\_\_

## Table 10.1  Popular Target Rounds

| Round | Number of arrows per distance | Size of face | Number of arrows/end | Perfect score | Age group |
|---|---|---|---|---|---|
| FITA Men | 36 at 90 m<br>36 at 70 m<br>36 at 50 m<br>36 at 30 m | 122 cm<br><br>80 cm | 6<br>(shot 3-3) | 1440 | Adult |
| FITA Women | 36 at 70 m<br>36 at 60 m<br>36 at 50 m<br>36 at 30 m | 122 cm<br><br>80 cm | 6<br>(shot 3-3) | 1440 | Adult |
| Metric 900 | 30 at 60 m<br>30 at 50 m<br>30 at 40 m | 122 cm | 6<br>(shot 3-3) | 900 | Adult |
| Metric Easton 600 | 20 at 60 m<br>20 at 50 m<br>20 at 40 m | 122 cm | 5 | 600 | Adult |
| Metric Collegiate 600 | 20 at 50 m<br>20 at 40 m<br>20 at 30 m | 122 cm | 5 | 600 | Adult |
| American | 30 at 60 yd<br>30 at 50 yd<br>30 at 40 yd | 48 in<br>(scored 9-1) | 6 | 810 | Adult |
| Columbia | 24 at 50 yd<br>24 at 40 yd<br>24 at 30 yd | 48 in<br>(scored 9-1) | 6 | 648 | Adult |
| "720" Collegiate | 24 at 50 m<br>24 at 40 m<br>24 at 30 m | 80 cm | 6 | 720 | Adult |
| Junior Metric 900 | 30 at 50 m<br>30 at 40 m<br>30 at 30 m | 122 cm | 6 | 900 | 12-15 yr |
| Cadet Metric 900 | 30 at 40 m<br>30 at 30 m<br>30 at 20 m | 122 cm | 6 | 900 | Under 12 yr |
| Interscholastic Metric | 36 at 50 m<br>36 at 30 m | 122 cm<br>80 cm | 6 | 720 | 14-18 yr |
| Modified Collegiate, Boys | 20 at 50 m<br>20 at 40 m<br>20 at 30 m | 122 cm<br><br>80 cm | 5 | 600 | 14-18 yr |
| Modified Collegiate, Girls | 20 at 40 m<br>20 at 30 m<br>20 at 20 m | 122 cm<br><br>80 cm | 5 | 600 | 14-18 yr |

| Round | Number of arrows per distance | Size of face | Number of arrows/end | Perfect score | Age group |
|---|---|---|---|---|---|
| **Junior Metric** | 36 at 60 m<br>36 at 50 m<br>36 at 40 m<br>36 at 30 m | 122 cm<br><br>80 cm | 6<br>(shot 3-3) | 1440 | 12-15 yr |
| **Cadet Metric** | 36 at 45 m<br>36 at 35 m<br>36 at 25 m<br>36 at 15 m | 122 cm<br><br>80 cm | 6<br>(shot 3-3) | 1440 | Under 12 yr |
| **Junior American** | 30 at 50 yd<br>30 at 40 yd<br>30 at 30 yd | 48 in<br>(scored 9-1) | 6 | 810 | 12-15 yr |
| **Cadet American** | 30 at 40 yd<br>30 at 30 yd<br>30 at 20 yd | 48 in<br>(scored 9-1) | 6 | 810 | Under 12 yr |
| **Junior Columbia** | 24 at 40 yd<br>24 at 30 yd<br>24 at 20 yd | 48 in<br>(scored 9-1) | 6 | 648 | Under 12 yr |
| **FITA I Indoor** | 30 at 18 m | 40 cm | 3 | 300 | Adult |
| **FITA II Indoor** | 30 at 25 m | 60 cm | 3 | 300 | Adult |
| **Modifed FITA Indoor** | 30 at 18 m | 80 cm | 3 | 300 | 14-18 yr |
| **NAA 300 Indoor** | 60 at 20 yd | 16 in<br>(scored 5-1) | 5 | 300 | Adult |
| **Chicago Indoor** | 96 at 20 yd | 16 in<br>(scored 9-1) | 6 | 864 | Adult |

**Table 10.1 Popular Target Rounds**

# DRILLS

## 1. Scoring by End

On p. 136 are four targets with the location of shot arrows marked by dots. At the right of the targets are two scorecards. Place the value of each arrow in the appropriate space on the top scorecard, with the arrows of greater value to the left. You should also indicate the number of hits, or arrows striking the target face, as well as the total score for the end and the running score as additional ends are shot. Double-check your score by adding the column of end scores and comparing the result with the running score. Compare the top scorecard to the completed one below it.

End 1: One arrow missed the target.

End 2: One arrow bounced out of the target and was witnessed by another archer.

End 3: One arrow skipped into the 2 ring after striking the ground and another is embedded in the arrow in the 9 ring.

End 4: Seven arrows are in the target face.

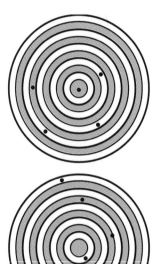

| E n d | Scorecard | | | | | | Hits | End Score | Running Score |
|---|---|---|---|---|---|---|---|---|---|
| 1 | | | | | | | | | |
| 2 | | | | | | | | | |
| 3 | | | | | | | | | |
| 4 | | | | | | | | | |

Total: _____ _____

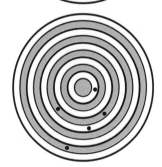

| E n d | Scorecard | | | | | | Hits | End Score | Running Score |
|---|---|---|---|---|---|---|---|---|---|
| 1 | 10 | 7 | 5 | 4 | 3 | 0 | 5 | 29 | 29 |
| 2 | 9 | 7 | 6 | 5 | 4 | 1 | 6 | 32 | 61 |
| 3 | 9 | 9 | 6 | 6 | 5 | 0 | 5 | 35 | 96 |
| 4 | 8 | 8 | 8 | 6 | 6 | 6 | 6 | 42 | 138 |

Total: 22 138

**Success Goal** = Score 4 ends correctly ____

**Success Check**

• If too many arrows shot, highest value dropped ____

• Bounce outs count for seven points; skip-ins count for zero points ____

• Any arrow embedded in another arrow takes the same value ____

## 2. Modified Metric 900 Round

Shoot a modification of the Metric 900 round, using the distances of 40, 30, and 20 meters rather than the official distances. Consult table 10.1 to find the target face size and the number of arrows shot at each distance. You can have the option of retrieving and scoring your arrows after shooting six arrows or after shooting three arrows. You can shoot your score alone or with a group of archers. If you shoot with a group, decide who will call the arrow values on a target, who will score, and so on, as described earlier. You should also follow the scoring rules given earlier in this step. One archer can control the shooting line as described in this step. Record your score on the scorecard at the right.

**Success Goal** = Complete a modified Metric 900 round ____

**Success Check**
- Follow the scoring rules ____
- Record arrows of highest value first ____

**To Increase Difficulty**
- Shoot from 50, 40, and 30 meters.

| Name | | | | | | | | |
|---|---|---|---|---|---|---|---|---|
| Class | | | | | | | | |
| | | 40 Meters | | | | | Hits | Score |
| | | | | | | | | |
| | | | | | | | | |
| | | | | | | | | |
| | | | | | | | | |
| | | Distance Score | | | | | | |
| | | 30 Meters | | | | | | |
| | | | | | | | | |
| | | | | | | | | |
| | | | | | | | | |
| | | | | | | | | |
| | | | | | | | | |
| | | | | | | | | |
| | | Distance Score | | | | | | |
| | | 20 Meters | | | | | | |
| | | | | | | | | |
| | | | | | | | | |
| | | | | | | | | |
| | | | | | | | | |
| | | | | | | | | |
| | | Distance Score | | | | | | |
| | | Total Score | | | | | | |

### 3. Interscholastic Metric Round

Shoot an Interscholastic Metric round from 40 and 30 meters rather than 50 and 30 meters. Note that you need two different size target faces for this round (see table 10.1). Follow the scoring rules listed earlier. Again, you can shoot alone or with a group. Members of the group should act as target captain, scorer, and tournament officials as mutually decided upon.

**Success Goal** = Complete a modified Interscholastic Metric round ___

**Success Check**
- Have your sight settings beforehand ___
- Check your equipment beforehand ___
- Use your personal mental checklist (see step 7) ___

**To Increase Difficulty**
- Shoot from 50 and 30 meters.

**To Decrease Difficulty**
- Use the larger target face at both distances.

| Name | | | | | | | |
|---|---|---|---|---|---|---|---|
| Class | | | | | | | |
| | | | | 40 Meters | | Hits | Score |
| | | | | | | | |
| | | | | | | | |
| | | | | | | | |
| | | | | | | | |
| | | | | | | | |
| | | | | | | | |
| | | | | | | | |
| | | Distance Score | | | | | |
| | | | 30 Meters | | | | |
| | | | | | | | |
| | | | | | | | |
| | | | | | | | |
| | | | | | | | |
| | | | | | | | |
| | | | | | | | |
| | | Distance Score | | | | | |
| | | Total Score | | | | | |

### 4. Head-to-Head Shoot

Find three other archers and have everyone put their name in a hat. Draw out two names; these archers should shoot against each other, as should the remaining two. Shoot four ends of three arrows each. The winners from each pair should then shoot against one another. The remaining archers can determine a third-place finisher.

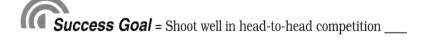

**Success Goal** = Shoot well in head-to-head competition ___

**Success Check**
- Relax hands ___
- Focus on target ___
- Block out other shooters ___

**To Increase Difficulty**
- One archer in each pair, as determined by the flip of a coin, starts with a two-point advantage.

## 5. Pressure Shooting

Archers often place extra pressure on themselves in head-to-head shooting by focusing on the other archer's success, especially in tournaments where the archers shoot arrows alternately. A good practice for head-to-head shooting is to write the value of 12 shot arrows on small pieces of paper. Make the total value equal to your average score for 12 arrows. Now shoot four ends of three arrows each, but before each shot, pull out a piece of paper and read the number. Imagine that this number is the value of the arrow just shot by your opponent.

**Success Goal** = Shoot at least your average ___

**Success Check**
- Use personal checklist (see step 7) ___
- Block out distracting thoughts ___
- Focus on aiming ___

**To Increase Difficulty**
- Write higher arrow values on the 12 papers.

**To Decrease Difficulty**
- Write lower arrow values on the 12 papers.

## 6. Time Pressure

Many tournaments establish a length of time during which archers must shoot all the arrows in an end. To prepare for the pressure of shooting with a clock, practice shooting three-arrow ends in 2 1/2 minutes.

**Success Goal** = Execute good shots within the time allotted ___

**Success Check**
- Relax hands ___
- Focus on aiming ___

**To Increase Difficulty**
- Shoot with a 2-minute time limit.

## COMPETITIVE SHOOTING SUCCESS SUMMARY

To succeed in tournament shooting, you must prepare carefully, cooperate to score accurately, and follow the tournament rules, as outlined in figures 10.1 and 10.3. After shooting a tournament round, you have a record of your personal performance, a personal record to improve upon in future tournament rounds. Perhaps you have already made new friends through your archery activities. If so, you know now that archery is a sport for everyone. It is an activity for the individual and the family, for men and for women, for children and older adults, for the advantaged and disadvantaged. Even though you may be grouped with like competitors with like equipment, remember that the challenge of archery always remains within the self. There is really only you, your equipment, and the target. It matters little what other competitors and tournament officials do. On each and every arrow, you bring your mental and physical skills to the test.

# RATING YOUR PROGRESS

Each activity you completed in this book had a success goal that prompted your development of physical and mental skills. The following inventory enables you to rate your overall progress. Read the items carefully and respond to them thoughtfully.

## Physical Skills

The first general success goal in an archery course is acquiring the physical skills to shoot. How well did you learn these aspects of shooting?

| | Very Good | Good | Okay | Poor |
|---|---|---|---|---|
| **Technique** | | | | |
| Stance | _____ | _____ | _____ | _____ |
| Alignment | _____ | _____ | _____ | _____ |
| Anchor | _____ | _____ | _____ | _____ |
| Bow hand | _____ | _____ | _____ | _____ |
| Aiming | _____ | _____ | _____ | _____ |
| Release | _____ | _____ | _____ | _____ |
| Follow-through | _____ | _____ | _____ | _____ |
| **Sighting** | | | | |
| Adjusting for windage | _____ | _____ | _____ | _____ |
| Adjusting for elevation | _____ | _____ | _____ | _____ |
| Adjusting for various distances | _____ | _____ | _____ | _____ |
| Shooting accuracy at short distances | _____ | _____ | _____ | _____ |
| Shooting accuracy at long distances | _____ | _____ | _____ | _____ |
| Adjusting and using accessories | _____ | _____ | _____ | _____ |
| Detecting your errors | _____ | _____ | _____ | _____ |
| Correcting your errors | _____ | _____ | _____ | _____ |
| Tournament procedures | _____ | _____ | _____ | _____ |
| Equipment maintenance | _____ | _____ | _____ | _____ |
| Equipment tuning | _____ | _____ | _____ | _____ |

## Mental Skills

The second general success goal is utilizing mental skills to improve performance. This area is frequently overlooked, yet it has the potential to contribute measurably to shooting performance. How would you rate your ability to utilize these mental skills to your advantage?

|  | Very Good | Good | Okay | Poor |
|---|---|---|---|---|
| Concentration on aiming | _____ | _____ | _____ | _____ |
| Relaxation during the shot | _____ | _____ | _____ | _____ |
| Confidence in your next shot | _____ | _____ | _____ | _____ |
| Imagery | _____ | _____ | _____ | _____ |

## Overall Archery Progress

Considering all the physical and mental factors you rated above, how would you rate your archery progress?

____ Very successful

____ Successful

____ Barely successful

____ Unsuccessful

Are you pleased with your progress?

____ Very pleased

____ Pleased

____ Not pleased

# APPENDIX A: MAINTAINING YOUR EQUIPMENT

Over months of shooting, you will need to keep your bow in good working order, maintain your arrows, and sometimes replace parts and accessories. You can save money by doing the simpler maintenance yourself and leaving the maintenance requiring special tools and expertise to the staff of a pro shop. For example, you can often purchase a dozen nocks for the price that a pro shop charges to replace one nock.

You also learn more about your equipment when you maintain it yourself. You can see how changing a setup affects shooting. Then you can begin to customize your equipment to match your shooting style. Once you are comfortable adjusting and maintaining your equipment, you will find that these tasks are an especially rewarding part of archery.

## Maintaining Your Arrows

Straight nocks are important to shooting accuracy. A nock misaligned by a few thousandths of an inch can send an arrow six inches off its mark at 40 yards. *Note: If you are shooting carbon or aluminum-carbon shafts, you must use special adhesives and avoid heating the arrow shaft. Instead of following these directions, obtain a technical bulletin from the shaft manufacturer.*

### Replacing Nocks

Archers who shoot tight arrow groups often break the plastic nocks on the ends of their arrows. It is worthwhile to purchase replacement nocks in quantity and a tube of fletching cement so that you can replace your own nocks. Nocks vary in size according to the size of the arrow shaft. Table A.1 lists the appropriate size to purchase for your arrows.

| Table A.1 | Replacement Nock Sizes | | |
|---|---|---|---|
| Aluminum shafts | | Fiberglass shafts | |
| Shaft size | Recommended nock size (inches) | Shaft size | Recommended nock size (inches) |
| 1413 to 1518 | 7/32 | 1 | 1/4 |
| 1614 to 1816 | 1/4 | 2 to 4 | 9/32 |
| 1818 to 2016 | 9/32 | 5 to 7 | 5/16 |
| 2018 to 2219 | 5/16 | 8 & up | 11/32 |
| 2317 to 2419 | 11/32 | | |

To replace a nock, first use a knife to remove any remaining pieces of the old nock. Lightly scrape or sand, with fine-grade sandpaper, any of the old cement remaining on the taper of the arrow. Because repeated scraping can distort the arrow's taper, an alternative is to carefully heat the old nock over a candle. (Do not place the arrow in an open flame.) When the nock begins to melt, remove it with pliers. Wipe the nock area with acetone, methyl ethyl ketone (MEK), or metal conditioner to get a good bond. Avoid touching the area because your fingers will deposit oil on the shaft.

Place a drop of fletching cement on the taper. Rotate the shaft as you spread the cement evenly around the arrow with your finger. Place the new nock on the arrow and turn the nock several times counterclockwise to further spread the cement. Rotate the nock clockwise with a slight downward pressure and align it approximately at right angles to the index feather (see figure A.1). Wipe off any excess cement oozing from under the nock.

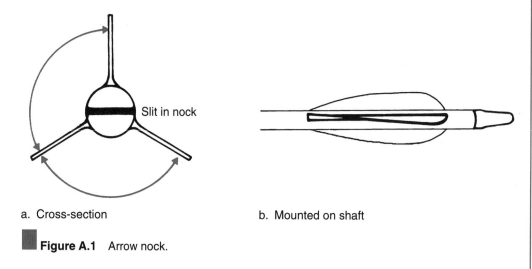

Slit in nock

a. Cross-section

b. Mounted on shaft

**Figure A.1** Arrow nock.

Place the arrow on a table with the index feather up. If the nock is on properly, you should not see either side of the nock when you look directly down on it from above. Adjust the nock if necessary before the cement sets. This is the standard nock position. Some archers, though, rotate their nocks slightly to achieve feather or vane clearance of the bow if they do not get the effect they desire with the standard position.

Another test of nock straightness is to roll the shaft on a smooth table with the fletching hanging off the table. Watch the nock to make sure its rotation doesn't have a wobbly appearance. You can also test nock straightness by resting the shaft on the fingernails of your thumb and middle finger with the arrow point in against the palm of your other hand and blowing against the fletching. The arrow will spin, so you can watch for any wobbling of the nock. Adjust the nock if necessary before the cement sets. Stand the arrow up to allow the cement to dry.

An alternative to gluing nocks directly to the arrow shaft is to use an insert system. The insert is mounted permanently in the arrow shaft, allowing you to snap a nock onto the insert. This system makes nock replacement quick and easy.

## Straightening Your Aluminum Arrows

Straight arrows are as important to shooting accuracy as straight nocks. You can straighten aluminum shafts on any of several commercial straighteners if the shafts are not too severely bent. Most pro shops make a straightener available to their customers.

Arrow straighteners have two adjustable blocks, each of which has two ball bearing wheels. The arrow rests in the trough created by the two wheels (see figure A.2). For slight bends, leave the blocks at the ends of the straightener. For sharp bends or bends near the end of the shaft, move the blocks closer together. Raise the plunger and place the arrow underneath it and in the trough of each block. Starting at the point end, rotate the arrow with your index finger, being sure to position your finger on the arrow directly over the wheels in either one of the blocks. Repeat this action, moving the arrow through the straightener until you reach the fletched end.

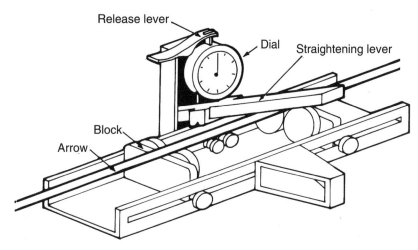

**Figure A.2** An arrow straightener.

If at any point the needle on the straightener's dial swings more than two lines, the arrow should be straightened. Find the place on the arrow shaft that yields the most needle deflection by rotating the arrow until the needle swings the greatest amount in the clockwise direction. The peak of the bend is now uppermost. Press down on the straightening lever. Rotate the arrow to see whether the bend has been removed. If it hasn't, repeat the process. When the needle deflection remains within two lines on the dial, the arrow is straightened.

Arrow straightness is important, so you should check your arrows frequently. To check your arrows when you are away from a straightener or are on the range after scoring, put the fingernails of your thumb and middle finger together. Rest the arrow shaft on your fingernails below the fletching with the arrow point resting in your other palm. Blow on the fletching. If the shaft jumps on your fingernails rather than spinning smoothly, the shaft might have a bend.

## Maintaining Your Bow

Most bows will shoot well for years if properly maintained. One key to maintaining a bow is remembering that laminated bows have layers of materials that are glued together. Extreme heat, such as that in a closed car on a hot, sunny day, can affect the glues used in manufacturing a bow. Prolonged exposure to moisture can affect the glues as well. Never lay a bow in damp grass. If you shoot a bow in the rain, wipe it dry when you finish shooting. You can help protect the bow by waxing it frequently with a special bow wax or other wax. Solid fiberglass bows can withstand heat and moisture better than laminated bows, but you should still avoid extremes.

Store bows in a case that lies flat or is hung vertically. In these positions, neither limb takes more pressure than the other. Standing a bow in a corner eventually weakens the lower limb. Recurve and straight-limb bows should be unstrung for any month that they will not be shot. Storing them in the relaxed position helps maintain their strength. Stringing and unstringing a bow with a bowstringer is better than doing it by hand because bowstringers put equal tension on both limbs and do not twist the limbs.

Compound bows should remain strung. Their limbs are not under as much tension as those of a strung recurve or straight-limb bow because the eccentric pulley does much of the work. If you are going to store your compound bow for a long period of time, however, you should unscrew the limb bolts in order to reduce the poundage. You may also need to lubricate your compound bow periodically. Usually the bow manufacturer gives specific instructions on how to do this and what lubricant to use. Most pro shops also provide this service. You also need to have the cables on a compound bow replaced periodically. Archers shooting four or more times per week often replace their cables every 12 to 18 months.

## Caring for Your Bowstrings

Bowstrings deserve your attention. Breaking a string can cost you points in competition because the arrow might not score well or at all. Waxing your bowstrings frequently with a bowstring wax minimizes fraying and wards off moisture. Waxed strings are also less likely to tangle when not in use. To wax a string, rub the wax on the string once or twice, and then run your fingers up and down the string for a few minutes to distribute the wax evenly.

You don't have to wax the serving on a bowstring. You should, however, replace the serving if it is loose. If the serving begins to fray during a tournament or shooting session, you can tie it off temporarily and replace it later.

Tournament archers always carry one or more backup strings with them. Because new strings stretch slightly when they are first put on a bow, the well-prepared archer breaks in backup strings by shooting them for a practice session or two. Tournament archers who use strings made of Kevlar often keep a log of how many shots they have taken with a string. Kevlar is known for its speed, but a Kevlar string breaks sooner than a Dacron string. Before a tournament, archers replace Kevlar strings they know are likely to break soon.

## Replacing an Arrow Rest

You must replace arrow rests periodically because they become worn or broken. To maintain good equipment performance, make sure the new rest is in the right place. If your bow is equipped with a cushion plunger, adjust the height of the new rest so that the center of your arrow shaft contacts the center of the cushion plunger. Adjust your arrow rest in the forward/backward direction so that the arrow contacts the rest below the cushion plunger.

If your bow does not have a cushion plunger, install an arrow rest that has a pressure point made of a flexible material, such as plastic. Place the arrow rest so that the pressure point is directly above the pivot point of the bow. Varying from this point either forward or backward usually magnifies the effect of poor bow hand position and torque caused by the bow hand.

# APPENDIX B: UPGRADING YOUR EQUIPMENT

You know the saying, "You get what you pay for." Why is this true in archery? Equipment that's made of quality materials and takes advantage of the latest technological advances performs more consistently for you. Just as your shooting form should be consistent, so must your archery equipment be consistent.

## Arrows

Good arrows are so important to accurate shooting that it is often said that if you give a skilled archer a choice between quality arrows and a basic bow or basic arrows and a quality bow, the archer would choose quality arrows and a basic bow. The best arrows are those that are consistent in the degree they bend when stressed a specified amount. This quality is called spine.

To see why spine is so important, you must understand how an arrow clears the bow when you release the bowstring. First, consider what happens to the bowstring when you release it. Even with the cleanest of releases, the bowstring rolls off the archer's fingertips and finger tab, sending it slightly in toward you as it moves forward. It then rebounds away from you, and then again moves slightly toward you as it reaches brace height. The string, being attached to the limbs, reaches its limit of forward movement and reverses directions, moving slightly away and then oscillating at brace height (see figure B.1).

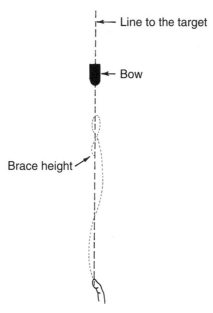

**Figure B.1** String path after release.

The arrow, of course, is attached to the bowstring at release, so the nock end of the arrow moves toward you with the bowstring. At the same time, the full forward force of the bow's stored energy is transferred through the string to the arrow. The point end of the arrow, resting against the bow, pushes outward against it. The bow resists this push. The arrow center is free to bend between the two pressure points. It first bends slightly to the right of a direct line to the target (see figure B.2). As the arrow continues forward, the center of the shaft bends to the left, in an equal and opposite reaction to the first bend. The shaft is bending around the bow handle at this point. Just as the fletching approaches the bow handle, the shaft bends to the right once more and moves the fletching away from the arrow rest and bow handle. In effect, the arrow bends around the bow without touching it. This action is often termed the archer's paradox. The arrow continues toward the target, alternately bending right and left in decreasing amounts until it straightens out about 10 yards in front of the bow and flies on line to the target.

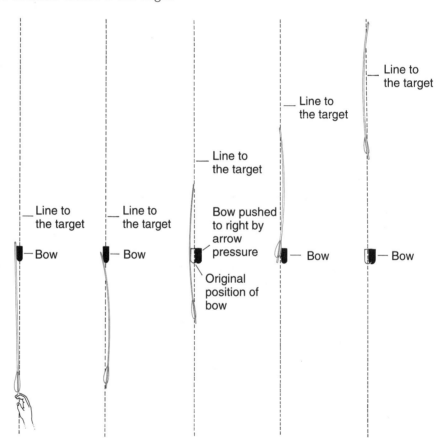

**Figure B.2** The *archer's paradox*: how an arrow clears the bow.

In light of how arrows clear the bow, they must have two qualities. First, the spine must be just right for your draw length and bow weight so that the arrow fletching clears the bow handle without contact. Second, every arrow you shoot must have the same spine. Arrows do not group, no matter how good your form is, unless their spine is identical. An advantage to the mechanical release aid is that the bowstring does not roll off the fingers. Deflection of the string is minimized, although arrows sometimes bend downward upon release with a release aid.

For serious archers, aluminum, carbon, or aluminum-carbon are the arrows of choice. You can be very selective in matching arrow spine to your draw length and weight. Aluminum shafts are available in several alloys. The more expensive varieties are the strongest and do not bend on impact as easily as others. Competitive archers use one of the top-grade aluminum alloys. Even if you do not compete, you may want to invest in arrows of this quality for both their consistency and their durability.

Some competitive archers use carbon arrows or aluminum arrows wrapped with a thin layer of carbon fibers. This type of arrow allows you to use a lighter, stiffer shaft that is faster and more resistant to the effects of crosswind than an aluminum arrow. Its chief advantage comes in outdoor shooting at long distances.

You also can choose from a variety of arrow nock styles. Which one you use is a matter of preference, but it should be a snap-on nock. A snap-on nock lightly holds the arrow on the bowstring and minimizes the chances of a dry fire (releasing the string with the arrow having slipped off). However, the nock should not be too tight, especially with light poundage bows. Test your nocks by holding your bow horizontally and snapping an arrow onto the string so that it hangs down. Tap the string an inch or two from the arrow. The arrow should fall off. If it does not, change the nock size or the thickness of the center serving on your bowstring.

## Bows

If you are serious about participating in some form of archery, you should have your own bow. The bow itself can be matched to you for draw weight and for bow or draw length. Also, the bow can be set up, or tuned, specifically for you. A good rule of thumb is to buy the best bow you can afford that is commensurate with your interest in the sport.

An important consideration in purchasing a bow is to look for a bow that is center shot. A center shot bow has a bow window cut into the handle and allows the drawn arrow to sit at a point close to or at the center line of the limbs. A bow without a window puts the arrow in a position where it is pointed significantly to the side. Even allowing for the archer's paradox effect of the arrow bending around the bow, an archer with a bow without a window must aim allowing for the arrow to fly off-center. A center shot bow overcomes this problem. An arrow of appropriate spine can compensate for the slight offset from center through the archer's paradox effect.

Center shot bows must necessarily be wood bows that are laminated, usually with layers of fiberglass on the face and back of the bow, or be bows with metal handle risers. A simple wood bow would not be strong enough if a bow window were cut into the handle. Most quality bows today have metal handle risers, often made of magnesium, because they are strong enough to withstand the forces to which they are subjected in shooting even when cut exactly center shot (see figure B.3). You can find both recurve and compound bows with metal handle risers.

Bows with metal handle risers have detachable limbs that can be of a variety of materials. Most have a wood core and a layer of fiberglass on both sides. Higher quality limbs can have multilaminated wood cores. The fiberglass layers provide strength, durability, and shooting speed. Through modern technology, bow manufacturers are able to offer bow limbs of other materials as well. These limbs can have a carbon layer with a foam core or be made of solid fiberglass. Each type has its advantages and disadvantages. A relatively new archer considering a purchase should ask about these advantages and disadvantages with an eye toward consistent performance and durability.

Bows with detachable limbs allow the archer to replace the limbs without having to purchase an entirely new bow. Recurve bows can be taken apart for easy transportation, too, and frequently are called take-down bows for this reason. Compound bows are usually left assembled, but the advantage of a compound bow's metal riser/limb construction is that you

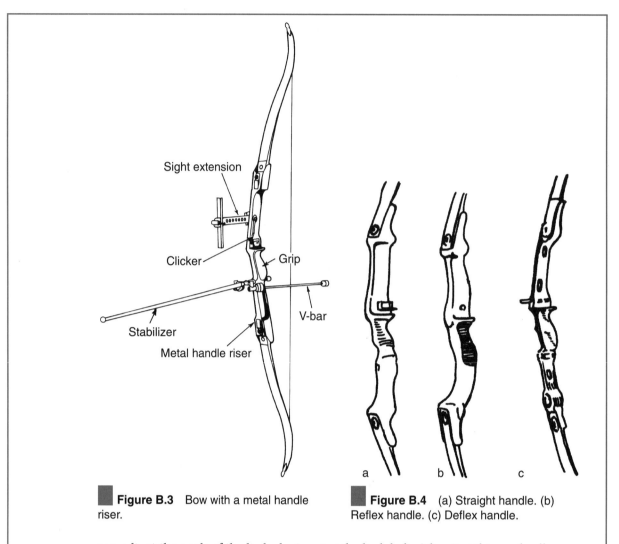

**Figure B.3** Bow with a metal handle riser.

**Figure B.4** (a) Straight handle. (b) Reflex handle. (c) Deflex handle.

can adjust the angle of the limbs by turning the limb bolt. Adjusting this angle allows you to adjust the draw weight of a compound bow, typically through a 15-pound range.

Many types of compound bows are available today. They vary in handle, eccentric wheel, and cable design. Compound bow handles can be straight, reflex, or deflex (see figure B.4). The straight handle is the most common. The reflex handle places the grip behind the limb fulcrum points, where the limbs attach to the handle riser. The advantage of this design is that the nock of the arrow stays on the string until it is approximately seven inches from the handle, imparting more energy to the arrow and increasing arrow speed. The disadvantage is loss of stability in aiming because you can torque the handle right or left more easily.

The deflex handle has a grip farther away from the bowstring than the other designs. It is stable to aim and accurate, but it shoots a slower arrow than the other designs. You should avoid extreme reflex and deflex designs in choosing your first compound bow.

Wheel design, especially size and shape, affects how much the limbs of a compound bow flex when the bow is drawn and unflex when the bowstring is released. Round eccentric wheels provide a smooth feel as you draw the bow through its peak weight and into the valley of the force-draw curve (see figure B.5). Cam-shaped wheels result in the bow being at or near its peak weight over a greater distance in the draw stroke so that more energy is stored in the bow limbs. This energy propels the arrow at higher speeds. Eccentric wheels can be cam-shaped on one or both sides with the two-sided, or full, cam yielding the highest speeds.

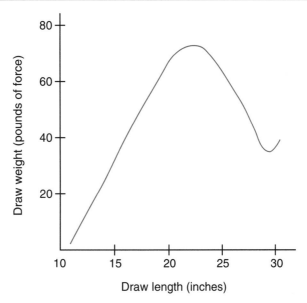

**Figure B.5** A force-draw curve.

Cam-shaped wheels are more common on hunting than on target compound bows because the longer period of near-peak weight and quick drop into the valley during the draw makes the cam eccentric wheel less comfortable for target shooting, where the number of arrows shot is greater, than the smooth, round eccentric. Full cam bows should be efficient, that is, transfer at least 70 percent of the energy stored in the limbs during draw to the arrow. Otherwise, they do not give you very much speed for the draw weight required.

Cables have undergone dramatic change since compound bows became popular. The first cables were steel wire. Wire does not stretch and is therefore consistent, but it can fatigue and break with prolonged use. Recently, fibers such as Fast Flight and Vectran have come into use as cables. These fibers are quieter and damp vibration better than steel wire. You can twist them to precisely adjust their length so that the two eccentric wheels roll over at the same exact time. These fibers can be cut by sharp edges more easily than steel wire, though. Improvements also have been made in how the string and cable are anchored to the eccentrics and axles.

Most bowstrings are made of Dacron strands. The number of strands is related to the bow's draw weight. A string of 8 strands is sufficient for 20-30 pound bows, 10 strands for 25-35 pound bows, 12 strands for 35-45 pound bows, 14 strands for 45-55 pound bows, and 16 strands for bows over 55 pounds. Choose a string with the number of strands appropriate for your poundage. Remember that more strands mean a larger diameter. If you have a bow relatively light in poundage and arrows matched to it, your arrow nocks will probably be too tight on a bowstring with significantly more strands than you need. Obviously, though, selecting a string with too few strands puts you at greater risk of breaking a bowstring. Bowstrings made of faster materials than Dacron are now available, but these are usually more subject to breakage than Dacron.

## Arrow Rests

For relatively little cost, you can add to the accuracy of shooting by upgrading your arrow rest (see figure B.6), particularly if you have been shooting off the bow shelf itself. Ideally,

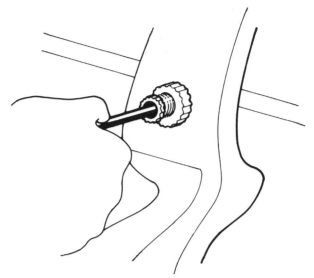

**Figure B.6** Adjusting the plunger.

you should have a cushion plunger or spring mounted on the bow window to absorb some of the force of the arrow when the string is released and the arrow pushes against the bow, especially if you are using fingers to hold and release the string. You can adjust the cushion plunger as to how far from the bow window it protrudes, which allows you to adjust the arrow in this plane as well. Springs typically come in one of several weights.

Arrow rests preferably are flexible. Some are spring-loaded so they collapse against the bow window if touched by the arrow or arrow fletching as it clears the bow window. The arrow passes to the side of the support arm of such a rest. The arm then pops back to its starting position.

There are also arrow rests available that require the bottom fletch of the arrow to pass between the arrow support arm and the handle riser. These shoot-through rests (in contrast to shoot-around rests) are typically used by archers shooting with a mechanical release aid. Because the release aid does not deflect the string as much as a release from the fingers, the arrow does not bend very much as it leaves the bow. Rather than the nock-end of the arrow bending to the side of the arrow rest, the arrow is on a straighter course, and the fletching passes between the rest support arm and the handle. Shoot-through rests can be used with or without a cushion plunger, but release shooters commonly use them without a cushion plunger.

# GLOSSARY

**actual draw length**—The arrow length needed by an archer, measured from the bottom of the slit in the arrow nock to the back of the bow.

**actual draw weight**—The energy required to draw the bow to the actual draw length, in pounds.

**address**—To assume a stand straddling the shooting line.

**aim**—To visually place a bowsight aperture over the target center; if a bowsight is not used, to place the arrow tip over a particular point.

**alignment**—With regard to the bowstring, the relationship between the string and sight aperture; with regard to shooting form, the relationship of the trunk and the arms.

**anchor point**—A fixed position against the body to which the draw hand is brought.

**archer's paradox**—The manner in which the arrow clears the bow upon release by bending around the bow handle.

**arm guard**—A piece of leather or plastic placed on the inside forearm of the bow arm to protect it from a slap of the bowstring upon release.

**arrow rest**—A projection from the bow window, above the arrow shelf, upon which the arrow lies when drawn.

**arrow shelf**—A horizontal projection at the bottom of the bow window upon which the arrow can lie in the absence of an arrow rest.

**bare shaft**—An arrow shaft without fletching of any kind.

**bounce out**—An arrow that strikes the scoring area of the target face but rebounds away.

**bow arm**—The arm of the hand that holds the bow.

**bow efficiency**—Ratio of the kinetic energy received by the arrow to that stored by the bow.

**bow hand**—The hand that holds the bow.

**bow scale**—A mechanical device that measures the draw weight of a bow at any stage of the draw.

**bowsight**—Any device mounted on the bow that allows an archer to aim directly at the target or a mark.

**bow sling**—A strap attached to the bow through which the archer slips the bow hand, thereby preventing the bow from being dropped upon release.

**bow square**—A device that attaches to the bowstring and lies on the arrow rest to measure brace height and nocking point location.

**bowstring**—The string on the bow, usually made of Dacron or Kevlar.

**bowstringer**—A device used to brace, or string, a bow.

**bow window**—The recessed area above the grip; the sight window.

**brace height**—The distance between the bow, measured at the pivot point, and string when the bow is strung; string height.

**broadhead**—A multi-edged sharp arrow point used in hunting game.

**bull's-eye**—The area on the target face with the highest scoring value, usually in the center.

**butt**—A backstop for arrows made of grasses, excelsior, straw, cardboard, polyethylene foam, or fiber.

**cam bow**—A type of compound bow with oval-shaped eccentric pulleys.

**cant**—To tilt the bow to the right or left, as indicated by the top limb tip, at full draw.

**cast**—The ability of a bow to project an arrow; the distance and speed a bow can shoot an arrow.

**center serving**—The wrapping thread over the center of the bowstring where the arrow is nocked.

**center shot bow**—Bow design wherein the sight window is cut out so that the arrow, sitting on the arrow rest, is at or very near the center line of the bow.

**chest protector**—A piece of nylon netting or vinyl worn over the clothing to prevent the bowstring from catching.

**clicker**—A device attached to the bow or sometimes the cables of a compound bow that indicates by sound that the arrow has been drawn a certain desired distance; most archers use its click as an indication to release.

**closed stance**—A shooting stance in which an imaginary straight line to the target intersects the toes of the rear foot and middle of the front foot.

**compound bow**—A bow using a cable system attached to eccentric pulleys mounted at the limb tips, producing peak resistance at mid-draw, and then dropping off to a holding weight less than the draw weight.

**creeping**—Allowing the draw hand to move forward immediately before or during release.

**crosshair sight**—A sight with a circular aperture in which two fine lines cross at right angles; the intersection of the lines is aimed at the target.

**cushion plunger**—A spring-loaded button mounted horizontally through the bow above the handle pivot point to absorb force as the arrow pushes against it upon release.

**draw**—To pull the bowstring.

**draw check**—A device attached to the bow to indicate that full draw has been reached.

**draw length**—The distance between the nocking point and the grip of the bow at full draw; at one time, draw length was measured to the back of the bow.

**draw weight**—The number of pounds required to draw any bow a given distance.

**eccentric pulley or wheel**—A round wheel mounted at the limb tip of a compound bow, used to decrease the amount of weight held on the bowstring at full draw.

**end**—A specified number of arrows shot before archers go to the target to score and retrieve their arrows.

**face**—The paper or cardboard with a target printed on it.

**field archery**—A type of competitive archery shot outdoors in a wooded area, with targets of varying distances and sizes; archers walk from target to target.

**field point**—An arrow point that is heavier than a target point and similar in weight to a broadhead; it can be unscrewed from a mounting insert in aluminum arrows so a broadhead can be installed.

**finger sling**—A piece of leather, plastic, or rope looped at each end through which the archer slips the thumb and a finger after taking hold of the bow; it enables you to maintain a loose grip.

**finger tab**—A piece of leather or plastic worn over the draw fingers both to protect them and to ensure a smooth release of the bowstring.

**fishtailing**—A back-and-forth motion of the nock end of an arrow on its flight to the target.

**fletching**—The turkey feathers or plastic vanes mounted on an arrow to stabilize it in flight.

**flight shooting**—A form of archery in which the object is to shoot an arrow for the greatest distance possible.

**flinching**—A form error in which the bow arm moves suddenly upon release usually flexing horizontally at the bow shoulder.

**follow-through**—The archer's position after release of the arrow; ideally, the body, head, and bow arm position are held steady, and the string hand recoils over the string shoulder as a result of continuous back tension.

**foot markers**—Anything used to mark the exact position of the feet in addressing the target so that the archer can duplicate the position and distance from the target on subsequent shots.

**force-draw curve**—The graph created by plotting draw weight (vertical axis) against draw length (horizontal axis) for a bow as it is drawn to full draw.

**full draw**—The position wherein the bowstring is moved back and the draw hand anchors with respect to the head and neck.

**glove**—A leather covering that slips over the string fingertips and attaches to the wrist to protect the string fingers and allow a smooth release; an alternative to a finger tab.

**gold**—The center area of the multicolored target often used in target archery.

**grip**—The part of the bow handle where the bow is held. Also, the removable plastic piece that allows a change in the shape of the bow where it is held.

**ground quiver**—An arrow holder that sits on or sticks into the ground; some also hold a bow.

**grouping**—The pattern of an archer's arrows in the target.

**handle riser**—The middle section of the bow exclusive of the limbs.

**heeling**—A shooting flaw in which the archer pushes forward suddenly with the heel of the bow hand at release.

**high anchor**—An anchor position in which the draw hand contacts the side of the face.

**high wrist**—The bow hold position in which the top of the wrist is held level with the top of the bow arm.

**holding**—Maintaining steady bow position at full draw during aiming.

**index feather**—The feather mounted on an arrow shaft at a right angle to the nock slit, often of a distinct color; the cock feather.

**kisser button**—A small disk attached to the bowstring meant to contact the lips in the anchor position to assure proper anchor and head positions.

**launcher**— A shoot-through arrow rest.

**let down**—A return to the ready position without releasing the bowstring.

**let-off**—The weight reduction from peak weight to holding weight on a compound bow.

**level**—A device attached to the sight or the bow to help the archer maintain a vertical bow position.

**limbs**—The energy-storing parts of a bow above and below the handle riser section.

**longbow**—A bow style popular in England in the Middle Ages; long limbs without a recurved shape are characteristic of longbows. Although not as efficient in design as a bow with recurved limbs, the longbow does not require the bonding together of materials, especially difficult in the past in the damp weather of England.

**low wrist**—A bow hand position wherein the hand is flat against the bow handle and the pressure during draw is through the forearm bone.

**minnowing**—Side to side movement of an arrow in flight, smaller and more rapid than fishtailing, and typically caused by the arrow's fletching contacting the arrow rest after release.

**nock**—The removable piece, usually plastic, on the end of an arrow with a slit for the bowstring.

**nocking**—Placing the arrow on the bowstring in preparation for shooting.

**nock locator**—A stop on the bowstring against which the arrow is placed.

**nocking point**—The location on the bowstring where the nock locator is positioned.

**open stance**—A position on the shooting line wherein a straight line to the target passes through the middle of the rear foot and the toes of the front foot.

**overdraw**—To draw an arrow so that the point passes the face of the bow. Also, a device that permits use of arrows shorter than the archer's draw length.

**overstrung**—A condition in which a bow is strung with a bowstring too short, making the brace height too high.

**pass through**—An arrow that penetrates completely through the target face and target butt.

**peak weight**—The highest weight achieved during the draw of a compound bow.

**peeking**—A shooting flaw wherein the archer moves the head at release in order to watch the arrow in flight.

**peep sight**—A plastic or metal piece with a small hole, tied into the bowstring, so that an archer can look through the hole to line up the bowsight and target.

**perfect end**—An end in which all arrows land in the highest scoring area.

**pin sight**—A sight using one or more sight apertures similar to a pin head.

**pinching**—Squeezing the arrow nock with the draw fingers during the draw.

**pivot point**—The place on the bow's grip that is farthest from the string.

**plucking**—A shooting flaw in which the string hand is pulled away from the face and body upon release.

**point**—The arrow tip.

**point-of-aim**—A method of aiming in which the arrow point is aligned with some point in front of and below the target.

**porpoising**—Up-and-down movement of an arrow in flight, typically caused by a mispositioned nocking point.

**post sight**—A bowsight with an aperture having a metal piece projecting vertically up or down, the tip of which is aligned with the bull's-eye.

**pressure point**—The place on the arrow plate against which the arrow pushes upon release of the bowstring.

**pull**—To remove shot arrows from the target. Also, to draw the bow.

**quiver**—A holder for arrows that may be worn, placed on the ground, or mounted on the bow, particularly when hunting.

**range**—The place where archery shooting takes place. Also, the distance to be shot.

**rebound**—An arrow that hits the target face but bounces back toward the archer, rather than penetrating the target; a bounce out.

**recurve bow**—A bow with limb tips that are curved forward.

**reflexed bow**—A bow that appears bent backward when unstrung; it does not necessarily have recurved limb tips, though.

**release**—Letting go of the bowstring, ideally by relaxation of the string finger hook.

**release aid**—A hand-held device attached to the bowstring used to draw and release the string, minimizing the string deflection otherwise seen with a finger release.

**ring sight**—A bowsight with an aperture that is an open circle; the bull's-eye is centered in the ring to aim the arrow.

**riser**—The center, handle portion of the bow exclusive of the limbs.

**round**—The number of ends shot at designated distances and target sizes to obtain a standard score.

**scoring area**—The part of the target face made up of scoring circles.

**serving**—A heavy thread wrapped around the bowstring at its center and on the loops to protect the string and to add strength.

**shaft**—The body of an arrow.

**shelf**—A horizontal projection at the bottom of the bow window upon which the arrow can lie in the absence of an arrow rest.

**shooting glove**—A leather covering that slips over the string fingertips and attaches around the wrist, protecting the string fingers and allowing a smooth release; an alternative to a finger tab.

**shooting line**—A marked line parallel to the targets from which all archers shoot.

**sight**—Any device mounted on the bow that allows an archer to aim directly at the target or a mark.

**sight bar**—The part of the bowsight to which the aperture assembly is attached.

**sight extension**—A bar that allows the bowsight to be extended from the bow toward the target.

**sight pin**—A bowsight aperture that is a straight piece of metal with a dot or ball at the end.

**sight window**—The recessed area above the grip; the bow window.

**sling**—A strap attached to the bow or to the hand holding the bow that prevents the bow from dropping to the ground upon release.

**snap shooting**—A shooting flaw wherein the arrow is shot immediately as the bowsight crosses the bull's-eye.

**spine**—The measured deflection of an arrow shaft, established by hanging a two-pound weight at its center.

**springy**—A small spring with an arrow rest extension substituted for a cushion plunger.

**stabilizer**—A rod-and-weight assembly mounted on either the face or back of the handle riser to help eliminate torque of the bow around its long axis upon release.

**stacking**—A rapid, disproportionate increase in draw weight in the last few inches of draw in some recurved bows.

**stance**—The foot position taken to address the target.

**straight-limb bow**—A bow with relatively straight limbs.

**string**—The bowstring. Also, to attach the bowstring to the limb tip by bending the bow limbs and placing them under tension.

**string alignment**—The relationship between the bowstring and the sight aperture.

**string fingers**—The fingers that hold the bowstring in shooting the bow.

**string hand**—The hand that holds the bowstring; draw hand.

**string height**—The distance between the bow, measured at the pivot point, and the string when the bow is strung; brace height.

**string pattern**—The relationship between the bowstring and the sight aperture.

**string walking**—A style of shooting wherein the archer moves the position of the string fingers on the string to adjust the vertical displacement of the arrow; no bowsight is used.

**tab**—A piece of leather or plastic worn over the draw fingers both to protect them and ensure a smooth release of the bowstring; finger tab.

**tackle**—An archer's equipment.

**take down bow**—A bow with detachable limbs.

**target butt**—The backstop for arrows, made of grasses, excelsior, straw, cardboard, polyethylene foam, or fiber.

**target captain**—The person at each target during a tournament designated to call the scoring value of all arrows on that target.

**target face**—The paper or cardboard scoring area mounted on the target butt.

**3-D round**—An archery shoot in which the targets are three-dimensional, lifelike foam and are placed at unknown distances to simulate hunting.

**tiller**—A measure of even balance in the two limbs; on a compound bow, a tiller is adjustable through the limb bolts, thus varying the distance between the base of the limb and the string.

**tip**—The end of a bow limb. Also, an arrow point.

**torque**—A rotation of the bow about its long axis upon release of the bowstring.

**tuning**—Adjustment of the arrow spine, arrow rest, pressure point, cushion plunger, string height, tiller, and nocking point to achieve the truest arrow flight possible.

**understrung**—A bow with a string too long, resulting in a low brace height and reduced efficiency.

**valley**—The point of lowest holding weight reached near full draw on a compound bow.

**vane**—A plastic fletching that is more wind- and weather-proof than feathers, but often is heavier.

**weight**—The number of pounds required to draw the bowstring a given distance.

**windage**—Horizontal correction of the bowsight setting to compensate for drift due to wind.

**wrist sling**—A strap that wraps around the archer's wrist and the bow, thereby preventing the bow from falling to the ground at release.

**X-ring**—A small circle at the center of the bull's-eye. The number of arrows landing in the X-ring is often used as a tiebreaker among archers achieving identical scores in competition.

# ABOUT THE AUTHORS

**Catherine F. Lewis**                    **Kathleen M. Haywood**

**Kathleen M. Haywood** is a National Archery Association-certified instructor who has taught archery at three universities. An eight-time Missouri state archery champion, she is now retired from competition. During her years of competing, she was a member of the Professional Archers Association (PAA) and the National Field Archery Association (NFAA).

A member of the American Alliance for Health, Physical Eduation, Recreation and Dance (AAHPERD), Dr. Haywood was presented the Scholar Award by the Central District of AAHPERD in 1995. She is also a member of the North American Society for Psychology of Sport and Physical Activity and a fellow of the American Academy of Kinesiology and Physical Education.

Dr. Haywood is the associate dean for instruction in the School of Education at the University of Missouri—St. Louis. She earned her PhD in motor behavior from the University of Illinois at Urbana-Champaign in 1976. A resident of St. Charles, Missouri, she enjoys playing tennis and watching all types of sporting events.

**Catherine F. Lewis** is an elementary physical educator at Andrews Academy in Creve Coeur, Missouri. A former member of the PAA and NFAA, Ms. Lewis has had more than 10 years' experience in archery instruction and a successful career in archery competition. She has taught archery in the professional preparation program at the University of Missouri—St. Louis and to youths in school, scouting, and camp programs.

Ms. Lewis is also a member of AAHPERD and of the Missouri Association for Health, Physical Education, Recreation and Dance (MAHPERD). She earned her master's degree from the University of Missouri—St. Louis in 1986. Ms. Lewis lives in Des Peres, Missouri, where she devotes her leisure time to camping, fishing, and reading.

You'll find
other outstanding
archery resources at

# www.HumanKinetics.com

In the U.S. call

# 800-747-4457

Australia ................................. 08 8277 1555
Canada ...................................... 800-465-7301
Europe ......................... +44 (0) 113 255 5665
New Zealand .............................. 09-523-3462

**HUMAN KINETICS**
*The Premier Publisher for Sports & Fitness*
P.O. Box 5076 • Champaign, IL 61825-5076 USA